P9-DGT-472

RECREATING
the
CHURCH

BOOKS BY
The Columbia Partnership Ministry Colleagues

George W. Bullard Jr.
Every Congregation Needs a Little Conflict

FaithSoaring Churches

Pursuing the Full Kingdom Potential of Your Congregation

Richard L. Hamm
Recreating the Church

Edward H. Hammett
Making Shifts without Making Waves:
A Coach Approach to Soulful Leadership

Reaching People under 40 while Keeping People over 60:
Being Church to All Generations

Spiritual Leadership in a Secular Age: Building
Bridges Instead of Barriers

Key Leadership Books

Gregory L. Hunt
Leading Congregations through Crisis

Cynthia Woolever and Deborah Bruce
Leadership That Fits Your Church:
What Kind of Pastor for What Kind of Congregation

Penny Long Marler, D. Bruce Roberts, Janet Maykus, James Bowers,
Larry Dill, Brenda K. Harewood, Richard Hester, Sheila Kirton-Robbins,
Marianne LaBarre, Lis Van Harten, and Kelli Walker-Jones
So Much Better: How Thousands of Pastors Help Each Other Thrive

Larry McSwain
The Calling of Congregational Leadership:
Being, Knowing and Doing Ministry

For more leadership resources, see
TheColumbiaPartnership.org
ChalicePress.com

RECREATING
the
CHURCH

Leadership for the Postmodern Age

RICHARD L. HAMM

CHALICE
PRESS
ST. LOUIS, MISSOURI

© Copyright 2007 by Richard L. Hamm

All rights reserved. For permission to reuse content, please contact Copyright Clearance Center, 222 Rosewood Drive, Danvers, MA 01923, (978) 750-8400, www.copyright.com.

Bible quotations, unless otherwise noted, are from the *New Revised Standard Version Bible*, copyright 1989, Division of Christian Education of the National Council of the Churches of Christ in the United States of America. Used by permission. All rights reserved.

Cover art: Fotosearch
Cover and interior design: Elizabeth Wright

For more TCP resources, see
www.chalicepress.com

10   9   8   7   13   14   15   16   17

EPUB: 9780827232532   EPUB: 9780827232631   EPDF: 9780827232648

Library of Congress Cataloging–in–Publication Data

Hamm, Richard L. (Richard Lee), 1947-
  Recreating the church : leadership for the postmodern age / by Richard L. Hamm.
     p. cm.
  Includes bibliographical references
  ISBN 978-0-8272-3253-2 (alk. paper)
  1. Christian leadership. 2. Church renewal. I. Title.

BV652.1.H237 2007
262'.1—dc22   2006033391

Printed in the United States of America

Contents

Editor's Foreword

Inspiration and Wisdom for Twenty-First-Century Christian Leaders

You have chosen wisely in deciding to study and learn from a book published in **The Columbia Partnership Leadership Series** with Chalice Press. We publish for

- Congregational leaders who desire to serve with greater faithfulness, effectiveness, and innovation.
- Christian ministers who seek to pursue and sustain excellence in ministry service.
- Members of congregations who desire to reach their full kingdom potential.
- Christian leaders who desire to use a coach approach in their ministry.
- Denominational and parachurch leaders who want to come alongside affiliated congregations in a servant leadership role.
- Consultants and coaches who desire to increase their learning concerning the congregations and Christian leaders they serve.

The Columbia Partnership Leadership Series is an inspiration- and wisdom-sharing vehicle of The Columbia Partnership, a community of Christian leaders who are seeking to transform the capacity of the North American church to pursue and sustain vital Christ-centered ministry. You can connect with us at www.TheColumbiaPartnership.org.

Primarily serving congregations, denominations, educational institutions, leadership development programs, and parachurch organizations, the Partnership also seeks to connect with individuals, businesses, and other organizations seeking a Christ-centered spiritual focus.

We welcome your comments on these books, and we welcome your suggestions for new subject areas and authors we ought to consider.

George W. Bullard Jr., Senior Editor
GBullard@TheColumbiaPartnership.org

The Columbia Partnership,
332 Valley Springs Road, Columbia, SC 29223-6934
Voice: 803.622.0923, www.TheColumbiaPartnership.org

vii

Preface

This book is intended to speak to leadership in all three expressions of mainline church life: congregations, middle judicatories, and denominational structures. It is common to draw hard lines between these three, seeing each as unique and distinct from the others. Some even want to lay blame on those serving in other expressions for the difficulties they are experiencing in the expression within which they are currently doing their own ministry.[1] Nevertheless, while the function of each expression is somewhat distinctive, they struggle mostly with the same challenges and demons. Though leaders in each expression have a tendency to lay blame on the leaders in the other expressions, all of us are, in most regards, in the same boat. As the twentieth-century cartoon character/philosopher Pogo said, "We has met the enemy and they is us!"

The final two chapters specifically point toward solutions and strategies, but this is not primarily a "book of prescriptions." Rather than leaping into "fixes," I believe it is essential to first reflect on the challenges that confront the mainline churches and those who would lead them. It is the desire for the "quick fix" that has so often drawn well-intentioned leaders into dead ends, frustration, and counter-productive "solutions" that simply reinforce the obstacles to change. This is one of several books from The Columbia Partnership Leadership Series that seek to both understand the challenges and to address them at a deeper level.[2]

I recently concluded service as General Minister and President of the Christian Church (Disciples of Christ) in the United States and Canada. The title "general minister and president" is an indication of the dual nature of the work: pastor and executive. I served for ten years and three months. It was the most wonderful, terrible, and demanding experience in all my years of ministry. I give thanks to God for the opportunity *to have* served in that role; I give thanks to God I am *no longer* serving in that role; and I give thanks to my wife, family, and friends for not leaving me *while* I was serving in that role!

The role of general minister and president, shared by the Christian Church (Disciples of Christ) and the United Church of Christ, is parallel to similar roles in other mainline traditions, variously called: presiding bishop (Episcopal, Evangelical Lutheran Church in America), general secretary (Reformed Church in America, American Baptist Convention), and stated clerk (Presbyterian Church USA). Among the eight mainline denominations, only the United Methodists have no corresponding office. Many non-mainline traditions also have a similar post.

Before becoming general minister and president, I served twenty-five years as a congregational pastor and as a middle judicatory executive (Disciples and American Baptists call this a "regional minister," while other mainline traditions call it bishop, conference minister, or executive presbyter). As a pastor of congregations I served in various settings: solo pastor in rural and exurban settings, associate minister in an inner-city church, pastor-developer of a new suburban congregation, and senior minister of an urban church. My congregational experience is rather broad. As General Minister and President, I used everything I learned in each of these ministries and more. The learning curve was steep from the first day I took office. I am still reflecting on the experience, seeking to capture any wisdom I can and to make that wisdom accessible to others through writing, consulting, and coaching. At fifty-eight years of age, I am not retired and, God willing, hope to have many more years to be a part of the ongoing conversation and the ongoing *transformation* of mainline congregations, middle judicatories, and denominations.

During those ten years (1993–2003), not everything I had hoped for was accomplished, and not everything was done as well as it might have been. I made some mistakes, which is how some of the deepest wisdom is learned (this is called *redemption*). Overall, I feel very good about, and thankful for, what was accomplished during those ten years. If in these pages I sometimes seem to be trying to justify myself, laying blame, or being immodest or otherwise inappropriate, please forgive me and charge it to: (1) my passion for my own tradition and for the whole church of Jesus Christ, and (2) the powerful emotions, both positive and negative, that leading mainline church institutions today engenders.

Turning a church around, whether a congregation or a whole denomination, has been compared to turning a big ship. Big ships don't turn on a dime. When a big ship is up to speed, the resulting momentum can require many miles to accomplish a complete turnaround. Turning around a congregation, a middle judicatory, or a whole denomination takes the time and energy of many people working together with the Holy Spirit. But it can be done and, thankfully, we see some parts of the mainline churches that are slowly coming around in some important ways.

"Mainline" is, of course, no longer a very descriptive term for the eight denominations that are the primary subject of this book, since much that is represented in such a term no longer describes reality. Some have suggested "side-lined" or "old line." The most accurate description might be "modern denominations," since each of these communions was shaped or reshaped by and during the modern era, and since we now find ourselves in a "postmodern" era. But we must remember that the mainline denominations are not the only ones spawned by the modern era. Some others have grown in *reaction* to the very ideas that mainline denominations have embraced and embodied.

Recently, some have used the term "progressive Christianity" to describe the theology and commitments of those who have been rooted in the mainline churches and who are attempting to "fight the good fight" of the culture wars. But while the core values and theology of the mainline churches may lead to progressive thinking, these same churches have not often been very progressive *organizationally*! So, with others, I accept that "mainline" is the common parlance and that trying to change this moniker is probably a waste of time and energy.[3]

Meanwhile, the learning goes on. The work of transforming the mainline congregations, middle judicatories, and denominational structures from rather ineffective *modern* organizations to organizations serving faithfully and effectively in the *postmodern* era is just beginning. I invite you to join with me as I share some of what I have learned and am learning on my part of this journey.

My purpose in writing, then, is to help the reader explore the following: (1) reasons why the mainline denominations and so many of their congregations and other component institutions have declined so precipitously in the past forty years; (2) ways in which mainline congregations and denominations can and must change; (3) ways in which mainline leaders must change and can lead the way forward.

The fourth purpose is, I confess, my own therapy as one who has spent many years on the "front line" of this struggle, a struggle that often proves to be "crazy-making."

My primary experience has been in the mainline church, and the pages of this book reflect that fact. However, I believe that other American churches will find much here that is common to their experience and need as well.

I am grateful to the religion division of Lilly Endowment for all they have done and are doing to bring a new understanding of the church in North America. I am grateful, too, for the grant that helped make this book possible.

Historical Background

Different scholars of different disciplines define differently the beginnings of the modern era. Some date the modern era from as early as the fifteenth and sixteenth centuries when, in Europe, Copernicus, Galileo, and Kepler began the scientific revolution and when nation-states rose out of feudalism. Some date it from Descartes in the seventeenth century. Others use the late nineteenth or early twentieth century.

As I use the term "modern era" in this book, I date the underpinnings of modernity from the fifteenth century onward and I recognize the iconic year of 1968 as pivotal in the end of the "modern era" and the beginning of the post-modern. The "modern worldview" understands the universe to be a place that is physically and spiritually ordered by certain universal laws. Thus, if one can understand these laws, one can control outcomes and continual progress is possible, if not inevitable. Culturally, White Anglo-Saxon Protestant (WASP) males dominated the modern era in the United States.

The post-modern era, as I am using the term, has its roots in the early twentieth century as Einstein's theories of relativity grew out of philosophical notions that had begun to understand the universe in less deterministic ways than had Descartes and Newton. The post-modern era began in earnest in 1968 in the United States when the WASP males' cultural dominance was challenged and others began to be heard in their own voices and had to be taken seriously (especially African Americans and women).

Since 1968, there has been no single, dominant, social consensus in the United States. Rather, a variety of perspectives and interests coexist. Sometimes these perspectives and interests find common ground, sometimes they are at odds with one another. The absence of a common social consensus hints of chaos and makes everything harder, yet it holds the promise of greater fairness and justice. The culture longs for spiritual values and connection, yet has become completely secular in that it does not consistently promote or respect any particular religious view or tradition. This is a time of change that is so rapid as to challenge both the capacity and the very existence of our social institutions. All formal authority is in jeopardy. It is a time marked by confusion, anxiety, and hope.

The term "postmodern" per se gives us a clue about the fuzziness of these times. "Postmodern" reveals only that we are in a time that is "after the modern." It is a time of transition that may last decades (perhaps we have already begun a new era that we cannot yet name because we are standing too close) or that may last centuries.

Of course, eras do not begin and end overnight: they flow from one to the next over a period of time. Thus, much of what is yet modern remains within this postmodern era. Some modern ideas coexist with concepts that are quite discontinuous with pre-1968 ideology.

It is my hope that this book will help readers more clearly differentiate between the modern and postmodern eras, and that those who seek to offer leadership to the mainline churches will more fully understand the profound implications of these differences.

Modern versus Postmodern

Some examples of the profound differences between the modern and postmodern eras:

MODERN	POSTMODERN
Immutable physical laws characterize the universe (Descartes).	Physical relativity characterizes the universe (Einstein).
Linear, rational, symmetrical.	Nonlinear, asymmetrical, many focuses.
Nation states are the building blocks of the world order.	Ethnic groups, mass communication, and the market are the building blocks of the world order.
Office—particularly hierarchical office—grants authority.	Relationships grant authority.
WASP males drive broad social consensus.	No single, dominant, social consensus—great diversity and many voices.
Communication is oratorical, formal, and indirect.	Communication is conversational, informal, and direct.
Progress is inevitable.	Progress is possible.

Why Is Leadership in the Mainline Church So Difficult?

"We, who are many, are one body in Christ, and individually we are members one of another. We have gifts that differ..."
(Romans 12:5–6)

In 1993, I was in Dallas, Texas, for a final meeting with the search committee for general minister and president. I arrived the night before the mid-afternoon interview so I would be well rested. Some friends in town, Michael and Sarah, invited me to lunch. Grateful for the opportunity to relax, I met them at a local restaurant.

In the course of our conversation, Sarah asked me if I had experienced any dreams the night before. As one who seldom paid any attention to dreams, I had to think about it. I realized that, yes, I had had a dream the night before, and as it came back to me I reported it to Sarah. "I dreamed I was in a big house. All the doors and windows were locked for some reason and I smelled the strong odor of natural gas! I kept trying to get out, but I couldn't. It seemed the place was going to explode! That's when I woke up."

As the imagery sank in, the three of us together laughed uncontrollably for two minutes!

Why is leadership in all the expressions of mainline churches so difficult?

There are several possible answers to this question. Some of these answers may have to do with our individual inadequacies as leaders. We may not be very skilled; we may not adequately understand the organization we are serving; or we may have personal pathologies that "out" through our leadership in unhealthy ways and thus sabotage our work. These are all possibilities we must take very seriously and for which we must be on the lookout constantly.

However, another answer that seldom gets examined by either the leader or the system is possible, and it is time for all of us who love these institutions to take a hard look at this one. *The modern paradigms, which are the underpinning of our mainline systems, no longer work. Yet these systems and we who comprise these systems are loath to change much of anything about them.*

Most of us in ordained ministry feel or felt *called* to change things: to change the world in ways that will make it more just and loving, to change the church in ways that will make it more faithful and effective. Even as we take our ordination vows in a setting of celebration and hope, most of us assume the *world* will be resistant, but few of us suspect how resistant the church itself will be to change.

The modern paradigms, which are the underpinning of our mainline systems, no longer work. Yet these systems and we who comprise these systems are loath to change much of anything about them.

Perhaps our first clue comes as we are "installed" in a role in the life of a congregation.

Installed?

Dishwashers are installed. Parts are installed. But should ministers be *installed*?"

As a former church executive, I have participated in a myriad of installation services for congregational ministers, and for middle judicatory and denominational executives. These occasions nearly always feature a "charge" or a covenant of some kind between the person being installed and the people he or she has been called to *lead* (though *serve* is a more frequently used word than *lead*, which should be our second clue that the church will, itself, be resistant to change). They also include lots of language about "office" and about the "institution" being served.

As always, our language both *betrays* and *shapes* our assumptions. Doesn't an "installation service" sound an awful lot like what happens when we call service people to install a new appliance?

The underlying assumption, a *modern* assumption, is that the church is a big machine that requires certain parts in order to function effectively. Thus a minister is *installed* to play his or her part in the *ecclesial machine*. A minister is not installed to *change* anything, at least nothing important to the essence of the machine itself. The minister is installed to make the machine work properly *as it was designed*, to fill a place that was left vacant by the previous occupant's departure. It is something like exchanging a new fan belt for one that has worn out or broken. And as the guy in the commercial used to say, "Parts is parts!"

It is partly a throwback to the modern era when it was assumed that we could "organize evil out of the universe," or, to put it another way, "We can successfully do God's work of redeeming the universe if we just get properly organized." We inherited these modern institutions, as they currently exist, mostly from the World War II generation. Along with these institutions, we inherited the assumption that these institutions are, indeed, properly organized and therefore need little more than an occasional "tweaking."

Now don't get me wrong. I recognize and appreciate the power of institutions for accomplishing good things and helping hold us accountable to the good work to which we collectively commit ourselves as the church. The church does express itself institutionally, but it is more than *just* an institution. The church is called to be the "body of the living Christ," an *organism,* not a mere machine.

A living body has identifiable "parts," certainly. Yet those parts are not static objects that are installed like a belt, a pulley, or even a computer chip. The parts of a living body grow and develop out of the very DNA of the body. If a part dies or is "removed," a new part is grown by the body or is "transplanted" from another body. The difference is not merely semantic. An *installed* part is "bolted on," but a *regenerated* or *transplanted* part is, or becomes, one with the body. This means that as the body itself grows and changes in response to its environment, the transplanted part changes along with it and actually becomes a part of the whole organism.

Of course, it is important for ministers and other church leaders to stay appropriately differentiated. We need to know the difference between ourselves and the institutions we serve or we lose our ability to lead. We should neither "disappear into the whole" nor allow ourselves merely to be "bolted on" to an institution like a new water pump.

So how might a celebration of the beginning of a new ministry become a *call to service* rather than a mere *service call*? Even if you have long since been *installed,* you can use the occasion of the beginning of the service of new lay officers and leaders each year, as well as that of new staff people, to help educate the church to what leadership means.

On these occasions, use language that affirms the church as the body of the living Christ. Avoid using reductionist language that implies we are merely "throwing open the hood" so the new part can be inserted. Use language about leaders and leadership that recognizes that leading is a corporate activity, not something one person does *to* or *for* the whole. The rest of the members have a responsibility to support and to hold accountable all the other members, including identified leaders. Use language that recognizes that leadership is about empowering others to discover, develop, and use *their* gifts as well. Think about the language of the governance of the body you serve. Do phrases such as "functional committee" and "chair" appear? You may want to consider using different language that reinforces relational qualities of leadership rather than functional qualities only. For example, the word "moderator" is more relational than a word like "chair." "Spiritual oversight" is a more dynamic phrase than "supervision."

Nevertheless, changing the language alone will not transform the church. Simply changing the word "committees" to "ministries" doesn't *make* them ministries, but it is a beginning. Having a "service of commissioning" or "blessing" rather than an "installation" won't by itself transform an institution into an organism, but it is a beginning. The words we use to name and describe *do* help shape and reshape our assumptions and our way of being.

Back to the original question: why is leadership in the mainline churches so difficult? Even in spite of the eloquent *language of transformation* that may be employed in services of installation, my experience suggests that the system neither expects nor really wants the minister to transform anything. The minister is expected to engage in technical change only: change that fixes day-to-day problems in the system *as it is*. The system does *not* want the minister to engage in adaptive change: change that adjusts the design or function of the system so that the system is *itself* changed.

Thus, in modern church systems, a minister is installed to be a sort of governor: a governor is a mechanical device that regulates the speed of an engine to be certain that it goes along at a steady pace no matter what kind of a load is put on the engine. Said another way, the purpose of a governor is to maintain homeostasis in the engine, but a governor cannot change the engine in its design or its function (even if the function is no longer relevant to the work that needs to be done).

What if ministers were *sent* instead of *installed*? What if they were *commissioned*? To be "commissioned" means to be sent to serve the *mission* (not just the institution) and to be given the authority to do so.

In the midst of a basketball game, a team's strategy and lineup are constantly adjusted in order to meet the changing conditions on the court created by the opposing team's strategy and deployment of players. When a change is made in the lineup, a coach does not *install* a new player. The coach *sends in* a new player who is authorized to make a difference and who is *expected* to significantly transform what is happening on the floor through leadership and teamwork.

Does this mean that ministers should be given *carte blanche* to do whatever they want to do, without regard for any authority beyond themselves? Of course not. We remember that all of us, lay and clergy alike, are subject to the human condition. Clergy are subject to the authority of God and to the authority of the church that commissions them, in part to be a check on potential abuses of the authority granted them. Thus, decisions about how the church relates to the world and how it functions in fulfilling its mission must be made in ways that are rooted in *community*, not autocracy. The community must confirm the individual's discernment of God's desires for the church. This too must be done in a discerning way and not merely by simple democracy (more will be said about this). This is why mainline denominations ordain individuals only after the wider community of faith confirms their personal sense of call as legitimate.

What does it mean for a minister to be "commissioned" or "blessed"? It means that he or she is given the authority (and the responsibility) to help the community of faith discern what constitutes faithfulness and effectiveness *now* and to shepherd the community into that faithfulness and effectiveness. This is different from being *installed* to keep the machinery running smoothly, to keep the boat from rocking, to stay the course, to be certain that nothing and no one has to change in any deeper, more significant, and *adaptive* way. Yet it is my experience that the church in all its expressions usually means what it says when it says it is *installing* a new leader. This locks down the possibility of creative partnership, reducing leadership to a mechanical function only.

At this point, the reader may be thinking, "Hamm sounds pretty cynical."

Let me set the record straight. I am not an angry, disgruntled former leader of a mainline denomination who has no hope for these eight denominations that are struggling to find a new way of understanding their mission and new ways to carry out that mission effectively. On the contrary, I have great hope for this part of Christ's church, because God is still God, and I believe God continues to work for the redemption and transformation of these mainline churches.

I am, however, disillusioned. And this is a good thing!

Who wants to live an illusion? How could faithfulness and illusion ever live together? It is only as we are *dis*-illusioned that effective mission and ministry become possible.

I *confess* that I entered the role of minister with many illusions, probably including the illusion that I knew what was best for the church and the illusion that I was going to single-handedly change both the church and the world. Some of these illusions had to do with youthful enthusiasm and some had to do with arrogance. These are illusions with which we all have to struggle in the process of maturing as Christians and as spiritual leaders.

However, the illusion I wish to address in this conversation is *the illusion that the church calls us to change the church.* Ironically, it is an illusion created by *idealism* about the church and ministry, idealism that is held by both laypeople and ministers. It is an idealism that is often overtaken by individual and collective *anxiety* about change, anxiety that turns the illusion into *delusion*. As the word itself implies, *delusion* has an evil connotation, an insidious quality that threatens to sabotage worthy ideals and ultimately sabotages needed change itself.

Now we are at the heart of the matter: *anxiety*. The faithfulness and effectiveness of the church is undercut, ideals become illusions, and illusions become delusions, through the ubiquitous presence and power of anxiety. In the individual minister and layperson, it is the fear of death (what Paul Tillich called "ontological anxiety": the fear of being). In the system we call "church" (or in *any* system for that matter), it is the fear of change, change being one of the faces of death, change *requiring* at least *partial* death.[1]

Am I cynical? No, I am not cynical (though I confess I have my cynical moments about the church and about myself as well). To be truly cynical would be to believe that people do what they do to sabotage change primarily out of ulterior motives. While I have certainly seen self-serving behavior from time to time in everyone, including myself, I believe people sabotage change primarily out of anxiety—their own and the system's.

I have seen otherwise excellent leaders (as well as lesser lights) used by a system to protect it from change. I have seen leaders betray their own call, betray friendship, and betray their own ordination vows, all to protect the system (and themselves) from change. These leaders seldom recognize that the system is using them in this way. They most often assume they are acting in the best interest of all concerned (which is the beginning of their own delusion).

Yes, I confess that I have often deluded myself in this very same way.

Thus, I do not regard myself as a cynic. Rather, I regard myself as having learned (often the hard way) that the human condition and sin itself is alive and well and driven largely by anxiety. Thus, as a pastoral leader, I have come to see more deeply than ever our utter dependence upon the grace of God. This recognition does not lead me to cynicism, it leads me to gratitude for God's grace and, occasionally, it leads me even to repentance.

Cynicism is not a helpful or faithful response to the struggle with these "principalities and powers"[2] that are nurtured by anxiety. Cynicism merely allows us to excuse ourselves as Christian leaders from taking responsibility for the real, deep adaptive change that the mainline church needs. Cynicism becomes sin when it leads us to dodge and duck the deep changes we know are necessary for health, well-being, and vitality.

The mainline church today is captive to American culture in much the same way the Israelites came to be captive to Babylonian culture, but God did not abandon the captives then, and I do not believe God has abandoned the mainline church today. However, God *is* calling us to repentance—that is, to *change*. God is calling us to change that will help us be more faithful and effective in the current context.

This transformation is not a once and for all proposition. It is not even a destination where we will be able to catch our breath before moving on. Transformation is a journey, a way of being every day…until that day when the reign of God is fully realized.

Remember Peter's experience of the transfiguration recalled in Matthew 17:1–6.[3] For this transformation to be worked in and through us as individual Christians, as leaders, and as mainline churches, we must confess and forsake our penchant for building "dwellings" to contain the divine, and for yakking away while the Holy Spirit is trying to reveal what we need to know.

2

Technical and Adaptive Change

Mainline denominations can be remarkably resilient institutions. However, as is true of all institutions, denominational institutions and their component organizations (including congregations, middle judicatories, national agencies, and so forth) must be able to change in response to their cultural context and to adapt their mission, structures, and style to serve current needs in the current cultural context. This is the first premise of this book.

FIRST PREMISE: Denominational institutions and their component organizations (including congregations, middle judicatories, national agencies, and so forth) must be able to change in response to their cultural context and to adapt their mission, structures, and style to serve current needs.

Unfortunately, it is also true that most institutions (including church institutions) tend to favor homeostasis—"staying the same"—no matter what happens in their cultural context. This should not come as a great surprise since institutions are created in the first place to conserve particular values and ways of doing things. And, institutions are created by human beings, who themselves have a distaste for change even when it is required to avoid disaster or to respond to a captivating vision.

It is my experience in organizations that, over time, conserving *ways of doing things* tends to take precedence over conserving, nurturing, and extending *core values*. However, it is also my experience that it is *possible* for important core values to be served and preserved while organizational forms are appropriately altered to reflect changes in a cultural context. This, then, is the second premise of this book: though organizations have a natural tendency to avoid needed change, change with integrity is possible, especially in response to vision.

SECOND PREMISE: Though organizations have a natural tendency to avoid needed change, change with integrity is possible, especially in response to vision.

If in your heart of hearts you believe change is *not* possible, there is no point in your reading the rest of this book. We already have too many church leaders who have given up on the possibility of change in the institution they serve, too many who are just "going through the motions" while visions of pension funds dance in their heads. But if you have not become so cynical as to be unable to imagine that the Holy Spirit can yet "make these bones live," then read on. Needed change with integrity is possible, but it is not usually easy. It is difficult because, by both nature and design, most organizations tend to preserve their form and mode, even to the point of doing disservice to their core values. Military organizations often devote themselves to preparing for the previous war rather than for current threats. Church organizations tend to serve the needs of the previous cultural context. In the case of the mainline denominations and their component organizations, this means being devoted to the ways and needs of the pre-1968, "modern" (or "establishment") era rather than the current post-1968, "postmodern" (or "post-establishment") era.

A corollary to the first premise of this book, then, is that the mainline denominations and their component organizations were profoundly shaped by and for the modern era and must become contextually relevant again if they are to be faithful and effective in the current postmodern era.

COROLLARY TO THE FIRST PREMISE: The mainline denominations and their component institutions were profoundly shaped by and for the modern era and must become contextually relevant again if they are to be faithful and effective in the current postmodern context.

Previous to 1968, mainline denominations enjoyed a kind of cultural dominance or hegemony in the United States. From the eighteenth century on, the members of mainline denominations were the primary religious, political, and economic movers and shakers of American culture. Our congregations and ministers enjoyed special favor and privileges. So, for example, clergy were given membership in golf clubs, seats at the head table in public events, and professional discounts. Mainline Christianity was a norm in this society. With few exceptions, from 1750 to 1968 mainline denominational institutions were growing in numbers of participants and resources year after year.

After 1968, however, mainline American culture itself rapidly disintegrated, and numerous perspectives and subcultures rose to challenge mainline cultural assumptions. A cacophony of voices and perspectives, no single one of which is dominant, characterize this "postmodern" era. In the face of these kinds of foundational shifts in the cultural context, all institutions have been reeling and craving stability.

For all eight mainline churches, the years since 1968 have been traumatic. We have seen declines in membership and in contributions for denominational work. In the wake of such decline, we have often engaged in blame. We have been racked with self-doubt and wondered if there is some fatal flaw in our historical core values.

Typically, the first response of an institution to shifting cultural ground is to seek to do what has been successful in the past but to "try harder." This is a form of denial and, since 1968, "trying harder" has been the primary institutional strategy of the mainline churches. The result is a focus on *maintenance* rather than on *mission*.

Maintenance has meant the continuation of organizational approaches and structures that were created or adopted before 1968. These approaches are largely ineffective in the current postmodern era. Denominations have now reached the inevitable point at which such reactive strategies have lost even the *appearance* of success. Leaders in both congregational and denominational settings are experiencing high rates of burnout, while resources of all kinds have diminished to a point at which many mainline denominations are actually in danger of complete functional failure and demise. Increasing numbers of younger mainline members and ministers, already relatively scarce, have been abandoning loyalty to their denominational structures, which further accelerates decline.

In struggling institutions, problems of declining membership and finances, increasing conflict, anxiety, and so forth are often seen as caused simply by individuals acting out destructive personal traits or behaviors. However, while every system does have at least a few difficult personalities within it, these problems are profoundly systemic. That is, systems resist change and use individuals to affect the resistance. These individuals are most often unconscious of the ways their personalities and actions feed systemic resistances.

Technical Change and Adaptive Change

In the great sea of books on leadership and organization, none is more helpful, in my opinion, than Ron Heifetz's *Leadership Without Easy Answers*.[1] Heifetz directs the Leadership Education Project at the John F. Kennedy School of Government at Harvard University. The influence of this book continues to grow as people in various disciplines are finding the concepts presented in it to be applicable to organizational leadership in all sectors. The fundamental concepts themselves are profoundly simple.

As Heifetz defines the terms, "technical changes" are those "fixes" used to correct ordinary problems in a system *as it is*. "Adaptive changes" are those that address fundamental values and that demand innovation, learning, and changes *in the system itself*. A helpful example is found in the realm of heart surgery.

One can make the case that bypass surgery is "technical change." It is a matter of restoring the free flow of blood through "pipes" that have become "stopped up." There is a sense in which such surgery is very expensive and highly skilled *plumbing*. However, when patients undergo this very technical procedure, they are soon confronted by the need for adaptive change as well, adaptive change that will reshape their very way of living, change that they must undergo if they are not to find themselves in bypass surgery again. Those who are smokers learn they must quit. Their diets change: less fat, more fiber, and better nutrition. Regular exercise becomes a part of their daily routine. They learn to better manage stress, even if it means changing their line of work. They learn to pay attention to how much they consume, their quality of rest, and so on. In a significant sense, they become new people.

Because of the educational efforts of the American Heart Association and other institutions, we now recognize the connection between arteriosclerosis and lifestyle. But understanding the connection intellectually doesn't necessarily mean we are willing to make the needed changes or that we are not capable of the kind of utter denial that deludes us into thinking that these facts "do not apply to *me*." Thus, many if not most Americans go on eating too much fat and getting too little exercise.

As I said before, it is my experience that systems *love* homeostasis, keeping things the same. This is why those who live and work in systems, including our congregations, middle judicatories and national structures, are often quick to embrace technical change. "Fixes" actually help keep the *status quo* intact. *Adaptive* change has to do with seeing underlying issues and addressing them in ways that alter the fundamental nature of the system. This is deeply threatening to people whose anxieties are already rising due to the dysfunctions of the system.

Leaders across the life of the church often expend so much energy in technical change that there is no energy left (in them or in the system as a whole) for adaptive change. There is so little energy left that everyone becomes convinced that they have done all they can do and that no further change is possible.

When a leader is expending 97 percent of his or her available emotional and spiritual energy just to keep everything going, too little energy is left to hear or to think new ideas. The more sweeping the new ideas are, the more difficult it is to deal with them. When you have 3 percent discretionary time and energy, and someone brings an idea that will require 32 percent or even 12 percent, you just can't entertain that idea. I observed this phenomenon in myself many times. It wasn't that I didn't want to take the idea, or the person bringing the idea, seriously. I just couldn't. It was emotionally and spiritually out of my reach. Seen one way, keeping leaders chronically exhausted with maintenance and technical change is the "system's" way of protecting itself from the deeper adaptive change that is needed. Seen another way, it is the people in the system each protecting their position within the system. After all, if the system changes, who knows what it may mean? It may mean the loss of a job, of status, or of familiarity and predictability. Thus, our exhausting attempts at technical change have a way of "inoculating" us against the deeper adaptive change that is needed.

The problem is not that technical change is bad and adaptive change is good. There is a place for each. But while some technical change is almost always in order, effective leadership seeks to go deeper and to understand the adaptive issues, directing as much of the energy of the system as possible toward those. Otherwise, to use a phrase popularized by Bill Coffin, we are just "rearranging deck chairs on the Titanic."

In my own denomination, I spent a lot of time and energy seeking to downsize the Disciples' General Board from 225 members. Finally, shortly after I left office, the General Board was downsized to about 145. Is this adaptive change or technical change? It remains to be seen as the newly sized board works out its role. If it turns out to be only a cost-saving measure, it is technical. If it turns out to alter the way the board does its work and actually enhances its ability to perform its functions of holding denominational units accountable, then it will be adaptive. Saving money (technical change in this case) isn't bad, but enhancing the board's ability to function (adaptive change) is even more important.

It is characteristic of institutions in denial to engage only in technical change rather than in the deeper adaptive change that is needed. Soon the purpose of the denomination, its congregations, and middle judicatories becomes *survival* rather than the mission for which God called it into being. Even younger leaders, who have grown up in post-modern times, tend to be drawn into this *culture of survival*. Their own fresh generational insights and instincts, along with their skills and energy, tend to get co-opted by the declining system. As available resources decrease, leaders have to work harder and harder till they finally become burned-out or unable to see outside the institutional "box" at all.

Ten of the twelve tribes of Abraham's descendants lost their way and were eventually swallowed up by foreign cultures. In the Old Testament story, the Hebrews were called to transform Canaan into a place where Yahweh reigned. But the local cultures of Canaan and the surrounding kingdoms and empires of the Middle East and Northern Africa were seductive to the Hebrews. Repeatedly, the Hebrews compromised their own purpose, identity, and calling for the allure of those cultures. In much the same way, the eight "tribes" of Christians commonly called "mainline churches," who in the eighteenth and nineteenth centuries felt called to transform the American continent into a kingdom of Christ, became identified with and dependent upon the same culture they were seeking to transform. They were shaped *by* America as much as they shaped it. Thus, when mainline American culture "came unglued" in the mid-twentieth century, the mainline churches were, in a significant sense, lost. Ever since then, they have been singing their same old song in a strange land. They have lost and continue to lose many members who have become absorbed by the culture into other religious expressions and other pursuits.

If the eight mainline churches are not lost, they have certainly at least been *wandering* since 1968; wandering and wondering what happened. "Why don't the things we used to do work anymore?" "Why are we declining in numbers of members and in resources?" "Whose fault is it?" "Has God forsaken us?"

Exodus comes to mind, again. The people wondered aloud to Moses, "Was it because there were no graves in Egypt that you have taken us away to die in the wilderness?" (Ex. 14:11). It was an understandable display of impatience. The distance between Egypt and Canaan was perhaps two weeks on foot. So why were the Hebrews out there in the desert for *forty years*?

As one reflects on the wilderness story, the answer becomes obvious. The Hebrews had been slaves to the Egyptians for many generations, and slavery is much more than just an economic or political state. Slavery soon becomes a social, emotional, and spiritual state. After so many generations, slavery becomes *internalized*. Now it was time for the Hebrews to come into their own as a people; to become a distinct people who would be used by God to bless the world. God wanted no one to bring a slave mentality with them into the Promised Land! After forty years, the memory of slavery would be nearly eliminated. Even Moses himself was not allowed to cross the river into the promised land. Joshua would be the new leader.

The eight mainline denominations and their predecessors have been enslaved in many ways to American mainline culture. The disintegration of that culture culminated in the years around 1968, and so, if we twenty-first–century members and leaders of these eight denominations are all undergoing a kind of liberation similar to that experienced by Moses and the children of Israel, then we are nearly at the end of our forty-year sojourn in the wilderness and it is about time to cross the river!

We may not like to think of ourselves in terms such as "enslaved" or "lost," but I believe we do well to recognize that we have been, and continue to be, in cultural captivity in significant ways. Perhaps "lost" *is* too strong a word, but frankly, whatever will help us deal with our collective denial is worth thinking about. It is my hope to help the reader understand how the mainline churches came to wander into this institutional desert. Even more, it is my hope to contribute to the conversation about how they can move forward into the future of faithfulness and effectiveness I believe God wills for them.

As a former head of a communion, I have seen denominational systems at their best and at their worst. While the worst can be maddeningly frustrating and unproductive, I still believe in the need for connective structures and I still have hope for them.

My hope, frankly, is not rooted so much in my belief in people as it is rooted in my faith in God and my belief that God has not given up on the mainline denominations. Because of the core values represented by the mainline denominations, I believe that if these eight died today, God would immediately go about reinventing them because they *do* bring value to the world and to the whole body of Jesus Christ.[2]

Moving forward out of the wilderness depends greatly on effective leaders who are not easily distracted from those things that are most important. But staying focused on what is most important is harder than it sounds.

Heifetz speaks of the need for leaders regularly to "get up on the balcony"[3] above the hubbub of the dance floor. A ballroom full of swirling dancers is a great image to describe what it is like to lead churches today. If the leader stays on the ballroom floor, in the midst of the dance, he or she will inevitably get caught up in his or her own immediate part of the dance floor. We become focused on our dance partner, the music, and the steps. We thus lose our capacity to see who is dancing and who is not; who is sitting on the sidelines without a partner; or who is having fun and who is not. The swirling motion of institutional life, the lights and the music, begins to feel a bit like the Tilt-a-Whirl at a county fair.

To make certain all is going as it should, as it is intended, someone needs to be up on the balcony above the dance floor getting the big picture. Unless a leader finds a way to get a bigger perspective on things, he or she will get caught up in the commotion and be neutralized or co-opted.

I invite you now, in the next chapters, to get up on the balcony with me in order to see the mainline church (and all American churches for that matter) with a new perspective that understands and appreciates the impact of the larger culture and the historical context.

PART I

How Did It Come to This?

The "Perfect Storm" Confronting the Mainline Churches

In 1991 in the North Atlantic, a hurricane collided with a powerful arctic storm, *and* with a massive area of high pressure, forming a devastating package. The resulting "perfect storm" was so powerful that it produced waves a hundred feet high. The storm caught the *Andrea Gail*, a fishing vessel, in the open sea. Sebastian Junger's book *The Perfect Storm* is a riveting and terrifying account of what such a storm is like and what it means for fishermen at sea.

This is a marvelous figure for the ship of faith, the church, in a time when the world is experiencing rapid and drastic cultural "sea changes." The "Perfect Storm" that has confronted the mainline church in recent decades represents the collision of several elements including: the dramatic shift of American culture from the modern into the post-modern era, the increasingly obsolete organizational forms inherited from the modern era, and the fear that has turned us inward toward maintenance and survival rather than mission. It may be tempting for some readers to "skip over" the historical review that follows. But resist that temptation! One of the mainline churches' primary problems today is that we have not really understood the implications of the massive changes that have occurred in our cultural context, especially since the mid-twentieth century. While we tend to get directly to "changing things," our efforts to change things most often fail because we have not examined our *assumptions*, which by definition are unconscious and nonverbalized. Our most heartfelt efforts for deep, lasting change will fail if we operate out of antiquated assumptions. As George Santayana wrote, "Those who cannot remember the past are condemned to repeat it."[1] We need to take history seriously and to develop some common language and concepts. This will help us understand the need for change and to think through that needed change together.

3

The First Element of the Perfect Storm

The Hurricane of Change in American Culture

The "Perfect Storm" that has confronted the mainline church in recent decades represents the collision of several elements, including the dramatic shift of American culture from the modern into the postmodern era, the increasingly obsolete organizational forms inherited from the modern era, and the fear that has turned us inward toward maintenance and survival rather than mission.

Sociologists, historians, and other observers of society often pinpoint the year 1968 as the year in which the disintegration of mainline American culture was sealed, the pivotal year in the shift from modern to postmodern culture. Of course, every "era" is cumulative. That is, while each era eventually distinguishes itself in important ways from that which went before it, every era is also built *upon* that which went before. However, the changes in culture experienced by mainline institutions in and around 1968 were particularly stormy, profound, and, in significant ways, discontinuous with the past.

Christianity came to the United States from Europe with colonial settlers. In Europe, the Christian faith was legally *established*: that is, each nation had an "official" church that was legally sanctioned and supported by the government. This European mixing of religion and government meant that the dominant political forces often used the churches for their own purposes (and vice versa). Many immigrants came to the New World to escape political-religious oppression in their homelands.

As more and more Europeans immigrated, a strong sentiment arose for the legal "disestablishment" of religion in the American colonies. When the new Constitution of the United States was framed, disestablishment had become practice in most of the former colonies. The First Amendment sought to draw the line between government and religion more clearly yet.

The religious majority in the young nation was Protestant and many had come fleeing Roman Catholic persecution in Europe. These Protestants comprised most of the social, economic, educational, and political leaders in eighteen- and nineteenth-century America. While they generally believed in the separation of church and state (legal disestablishment), they nevertheless wanted the United States to be a Protestant country. Thus, they hoped for a kind of *voluntary, non-legal,* or *informal* "establishment" of Protestantism.

While most American church leaders in those nascent days of the United States recognized fellow Protestants as partners in the evangelization of the new nation, they also each hoped that their own communion would become the voluntarily established church of the land. Thus, fueled by a sometimes-uneasy mix of cooperation and competition, a kind of "Protestant Crusade" to make the United States a Christian nation began.

Though never achieving complete "voluntary establishment," these predecessors of today's "mainline" denominations did manage to achieve a large measure of dominance within American culture. This is precisely why these denominations came to be called "mainline."

Not only did the vision of a "Christian nation" have the power to stir passion and raise money for the building of denominational religious and educational institutions, the larger vision of a "Christian *world*" fueled a powerful missionary movement. By 1890, an estimated 5000 North American missionaries were serving overseas. Unfortunately, this powerful missionary movement had precious little introspection or self-criticism. It was often nationalistic, fraught with cultural assumptions and a kind of arrogance that assumed that American economic and political values were the only truly "Christian" values and that American ways were the only "right" ways. It has been argued that most American Protestant missionaries were as much missionaries of American culture as of Christian faith. It was not until the 1960s that the mainline churches began to respond effectively to these critiques.

American mainline Protestantism continued to grow in size and strength throughout the eighteenth and nineteenth centuries. However, beginning in the 1920s, the cultural dominance of the mainline denominations began to wane. The first cracks appeared immediately after WWI and began with the public's disillusionment about that war (lots of people killed, not much settled). Church leaders, as well as other social and political leaders, had publicly supported the war. This disillusionment undercut formal authority in the culture generally and in mainline denominations specifically. A second cause was the conflict within the churches generated by the modernist-fundamentalist debate. The two sides demonized each other so completely that many members left saying, "A plague on both your houses!" A third cause was the rising confidence in science, rather than religion, as the bearer of the answers to life's quintessential questions. Fourth, there was a mass migration of people from the farm to the city (which is always socially and spiritually disorienting). Thus, throughout the 1920s and 30s the influence of "mainline Protestantism" waned.

Beginning of the end of mainline Protestantism's cultural dominance

1. Public disillusionment with WWI and with the cultural leaders who supported it (including those of the church)
2. The modernist vs. fundamentalist debate
3. The rising confidence in science as the bearer of truth
4. The mass migration of Americans to cities

The national crisis generated by World War II (1941–45) *seemed* to reverse these trends, as many people returned to the mainline churches during and after the war. Attendance rose, and many new mainline congregations were started in the newly forming suburbs of the 1950s. However, the respite in the decline of mainline Protestantism was temporary and in the 1960s Americans saw the whole fabric of the mainline cultural consensus itself unraveling.

The "mainline cultural consensus" reflected a mostly Anglo-Saxon male Protestant perspective. If one were female, or a person of color, or a person of an ethnicity other than northern Euro-American or of a non-Protestant faith, one nevertheless had to accommodate this Anglo-Saxon male Protestant cultural dominance. But with the rise of the civil rights movement and the anti-war movement, the images of Sheriff Bull Connor's dogs, burning American cities, and body bags served up nightly on network television, this "consensus" began to come apart, and new voices clamored to be heard.

The year 1968 was a signature year in the disintegration of the mainline cultural consensus. In this iconic year, Martin Luther King Jr. and presidential candidate Bobby Kennedy were assassinated, the Democratic National Convention in Chicago was swamped with protests, a number of American cities burned both with fire and anger in the face of expectations raised by the civil rights movement and then dashed by continuing realities of bigotry and racism. In this same year, American involvement in Vietnam increased to 500,000 troops in a war that had no clearly stated purpose and no exit strategy. The deadly Tet Offensive overran American and South Vietnamese defenders and the My Lai Massacre (perpetrated by American soldiers) resulted in the deaths of many villagers, including many women and children. President Lyndon Johnson decided not to run for reelection because of the strength of opposition to the Vietnam War. Protesting students shut down Columbia University.

It was also in 1968 that mainline institutions of all kinds, including mainline churches, began to experience decreasing attendance. Some members went to other, *non*-mainline churches, but many left the church altogether. Especially notable among those who left altogether were huge numbers of Baby Boomers (born after 1945). But most mainline churches seemed not to notice, or simply hoped they would return, or didn't know what to do about it.

The disintegration of the "mainline consensus" was devastating to the mainline churches in part because, in their symbiotic relationship with American culture, *the mainline churches had come to depend upon the culture to convey the language and concepts of the faith for them.* Before 1968, children opened every public school day with the Pledge of Allegiance *and* the Lord's Prayer. In December, public school choirs sang Christmas carols. Spring break was "Easter Break" and always came during Holy Week. In some regions, public schools scheduled nothing on Wednesday nights or Sunday mornings because these were reserved for church activities. The curriculum was full of references to the Bible and to the mainline church. Upon graduation, attendance was *required* at school-sponsored worship services called "baccalaureate."

Television stations began each day with an inspirational Christian message and gave free broadcasting time to religious programs. The courthouse square hosted a manger scene, and the city utility poles sported festive Christmas decorations with Christian themes. The mainline Protestant churches were the place the culture said people should be (at least people who wanted to succeed and truly reflect the American Dream). It was not until 1960 that a Roman Catholic could be elected President, and the election of John Kennedy was due in large measure to Kennedy's meeting with mainline American religious leaders and assuring them that he would not make his decisions as President on the basis of the teachings of the Vatican.

The response of mainline church leadership in the 1960s and 1970s was mostly denial and a failure to understand what was happening. Why did mainline church leaders not immediately (in the 1960s and 1970s) understand what was happening? Because, it must be admitted, they were as deeply embedded in American cultural assumptions as most everyone else. Yet there are other reasons as well.

One is that it takes several years of statistics moving fairly consistently in the same direction before one can perceive or safely declare a trend. Early statistics of the 1960s and 1970s sent mixed signals, as noted below.

A second reason is that there was a sort of "demographic flywheel" effect. That is, adults were living longer, and the later stages of the post–WWII baby boom were still producing enough children to create the illusion that nothing had changed drastically. The presence of these later Baby Boomers (born 1955–65) tended to mask that the early Boomers (born 1945–55) were disappearing from the church in large numbers. The absence of these young adults was often blamed on a developmentally "natural" departure from church: it was thought they would "come back" when they got married and had children of their own. But vast numbers never came back. Not until the later Boomers (born 1955–65) left in the 1970s and early 1980s did church leaders began to look around and realize that many congregations were becoming alarmingly older in average age and that the average age of seminarians was rising fast as well.

A third reason mainline church leaders failed to comprehend what was happening is that mission offerings continued to grow slowly well after the decline in membership had gotten under way. Not until the late 1980's did mission offerings begin to be flat and then to gradually decline (this happened because the World War II generation's earning capacity did not peak until the 1970s). Frankly, dollar decreases were more immediately alarming than membership decreases to denominational bureaucracies. It was easier for bureaucratic leaders, who are the keepers of statistics, to engage in denial until offerings for denominational causes actually began to decline in a way that was *felt* by middle judicatories and denominational personnel. (I do not wish to be harsh or judgmental in this observation, but it does point to one of the dangers of bureaucratic styles of leadership.)

A fourth reason, found among some mainline church leaders, was an attitude that viewed the decreases as a sign that the denominations were paying the "price of faithfulness." That is, some mainline church leaders and governing bodies (especially in national settings) had taken unpopular stands in regard to such issues as racism and the Vietnam War, and so some concluded that a lot of contributing members just couldn't take the "heat" of the "truth." This was a self-serving, but understandable, interpretation. If we had done statistical analyses of who was still attending, however, we would have found that the losses were primarily among the young, not the old (who were the primary contributors and would have been more likely to leave than would the young when traditional values were challenged).

A fifth reason, undoubtedly, was a kind of pride in what had been accomplished by the mainline churches during the 1940s, 1950s and early 1960s. Much had been accomplished in terms of new congregations started, mission work done, institutions built up, and membership gained. The resulting understandable pride made decline too difficult to readily recognize and accept.

While these are five individual reasons, taken together they are all elements of a collective denial on the part of the mainline church. However, we should not be too hard on those leaders of the mainline church in the 1970s. After all, who can discern a major cultural shift *as it is happening*? It usually takes a decade or more for scholars to recognize such major shifts, so why would we expect church leaders to recognize it immediately?

Yet it must be admitted that denial persisted long past the time when it became evident that these statistical declines represented long-term trends, not just short "blips." Still, I would not characterize the continued denial as a failure of individual leaders so much as a *systemic* failure. Systems hate to change, and even very perceptive leaders undoubtedly got *captured* by cultural assumptions and by organizational dynamics that contributed to denial and to the maintenance of the status quo.

This "hurricane of cultural change" was the first element of the Perfect Storm.

Bad News and Good News

As we think about the "cultural hurricane" that rocked the mainline church in the 1960s and in the following decades, bringing shrinking membership and resources, our first instinct is to think, "This is terrible!" And in some ways, it has been terrible. On the other hand, the mainline church had become dependent on American culture to convey the language and concepts of faith, and thus the gospel became diluted and distorted in many ways by being confused with the nation's own story. Thus, like every storm, while bringing uncontrollable energy and chaos, this "cultural storm" "cleared the air" in some important ways.

It is also important to remember that the mainline cultural consensus was a White Anglo-Saxon Protestant male consensus that effectively silenced women and people of all other races and ethnicities. While the current absence of a cultural consensus is complicating in many ways, it is certainly more just and makes way for more voices and perspectives to participate in finding solutions to some of our most vexing social problems: many of which were generated by the monolithic cultural consensus to begin with.

While the mainline churches are just now beginning to figure out how to be and what to do in the face of the new postmodern cultural context, many of the non-mainline churches have yet even to acknow-ledge the reality of the shift as anything other than something to resist.

It is worth noting that the hurricane that combined with an arctic storm and massive area of high pressure to create the "Perfect Storm" was named Grace.

This brings us to the second element of the Perfect Storm that has confronted the mainline churches.

The Second Element of the Perfect Storm

Organizational Obsolescence

The "Perfect Storm" that has confronted the mainline church in recent decades represents the collision of several elements including: the dramatic shift of American culture from the modern into the postmodern era, the increasingly obsolete organizational forms inherited from the modern era, and the fear that has turned us inward toward maintenance and survival rather than mission.

I wish to address two kinds of organizational obsolescence here. One kind, which I will call "systemic obsolescence," occurs as systems naturally go through their life cycle and "run down." The other kind of organizational obsolescence, which I will call "generational obsolescence," comes when a particular generation reshapes the church in ways that suit their own characteristics and needs but do not permit or encourage the reshaping of the church in ways that successfully suit the characteristics and needs of successive generations.

Systemic Obsolescence

Social and religious movements, and the institutions they create, generally follow a path something like that in Figure 4-1. A successful movement typically begins with the charismatic and visionary leadership of one or more individuals who articulate a vision that "catches a cultural wave" of the day. That "cultural wave" helps to propel a movement just as surfers catch a wave that carries them along. However, if a movement is to continue beyond this original high-energy period, it must success-fully make the transition from movement to institution. To accomplish this, the original visionary leaders must be effective organizers as well as visionaries (an unusual combination of gifts in an individual) or there must be others who are effective organizers who come in to give organizational shape to the movement.

Fig. 4-1: An Organizational Maturation Curve

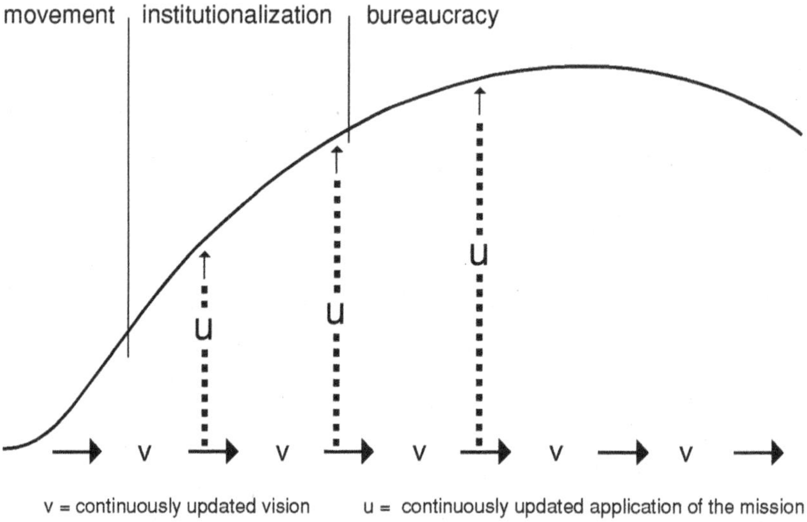

movement | institutionalization | bureaucracy

v = continuously updated vision   u = continuously updated application of the mission

In order for the movement to continue beyond the active life of the original generation of leaders, there must be second- and third-generation leaders (and those following them) who are effective organizers and can thus continue to "institutionalize" the vision of the movement's founders. History is littered with movements that died after only one generation, either because there was no one present who was capable of creating an institutional embodiment of it, or because the "cultural wave" it was riding fizzled out, or because no one discerned an updated vision or effectively updated the application of the original vision to keep it con-temporary and relevant in content and expression.

Many of us have known new congregations that died out soon after being established because the "wave" or "window of opportunity" in a newly forming neighborhood was missed, or because the organizing pastor was a visionary but not an organizer, or because succeeding gener-ations of leaders were not effective organizers.

Likewise, mainline denominations themselves were each driven by a founding vision and each rode a "wave" of particular cultural interests.[1]

These "waves" moved atop a high "tide" of mainline cultural establishment for many years. The significance of the individual "waves" began to be forgotten over the course of the nineteenth and twentieth centuries and the tide of mainline culture ebbed in the mid-twentieth century. National, regional, and congregational leaders often failed to discern an updated vision (line "V" in Figure 4-1), or failed to effectively update the application of the original vision (line "U" in Figure 4-1). Thus, the vision was not kept contemporary and relevant in content and expression.

As they mature, institutions (including denominations as a whole and middle judicatories and congregations individually) follow what may be called an "organizational maturation curve." Organizations of all kinds fall prey to what physicists call the "Second Law of Thermodynamics." That is, apart from intentional intervention, things just naturally "wind down" over time. Thus, institutions tend to follow a trajectory approximated in Figure 4-2.

Fig. 4-2: Church Organizational Maturation Curve

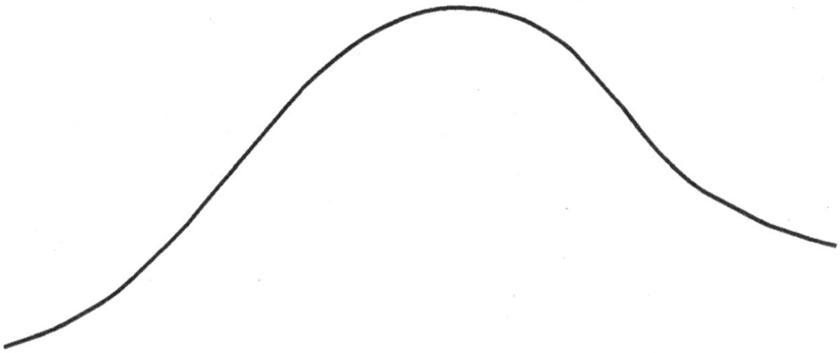

As an institution is successfully built, it grows in numbers, strength, and organizational sophistication. As time passes, the leadership updates the original vision and the application of the original vision of the institution (line "V" represents the continually updated vision and line "U" represents the continually updated *application* of the vision). Eventually, the organization reaches a level of organizational maturity that results in the creation of a bureaucracy.

"Bureaucracy" is a negative word these days, which is part of the anti-institutional legacy of the 1960s, 1970s, and 1980s. But effective bureaucracies are necessary to accomplish some things. Very large undertakings nearly always require some kind of organizational bureaucracy in order for results to be accomplished and maintained.

The question, then, is not whether bureaucracies are necessary, but whether a particular bureaucracy is functioning in a way that is more helpful or less helpful. For example, almost no one questions the need for FEMA (the Federal Emergency Management Agency), but many questioned its effectiveness in the wake of Hurricane Katrina. The challenge is that bureaucracies, like all human systems, have a natural tendency to become self-serving, mired in obsolete methods (ruts), and preoccupied with control instead of with serving the mission for which they were created. Decline typically occurs as shown in figure 4-3.

Fig. 4-3: The Bureaucracy Turns in on Itself

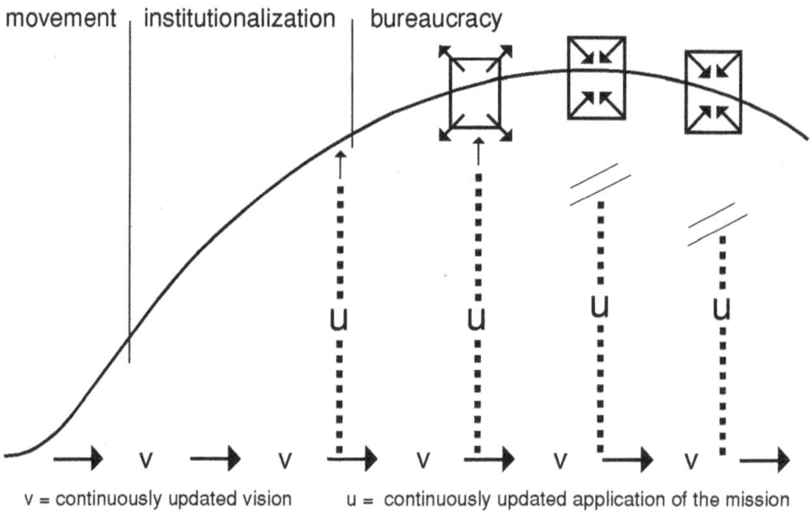

movement | institutionalization | bureaucracy

v = continuously updated vision   u = continuously updated application of the mission

The boxes on the organizational maturation curve represent the "bureaus" or departments through which the work of the organization is done (the enabling and implementing of the regularly updated vision/mission). The problem arises as those working inside these boxes become less concerned about the work of the organization than they are about "life inside the box." All of us have seen this phenomenon in governmental, educational, social, commercial, and religious organizations and institutions. As the concerns of those who are supposed to be leading in the implementation of the vision/mission become more concerned with "life in the box" (note the arrows that have begun to point inward instead of outward), the institution begins to lose its mission focus. The institution becomes self-serving, loses the confidence of the membership, and suffers decline. Every human institution, including every expression of the church, has this tendency to "turn in on itself" and to become preoccupied with self-service and survival.

It should be added that this is seldom a conscious process purposely perpetrated by mean-spirited people. On the contrary, even the finest people can be pulled into this dynamic precisely because it *is* systemic and not merely individual in nature. It is insidious and can be combated only with conscious intentionality. Understanding these dynamics and intentionally addressing them are among the most important functions of effective leadership. In the absence of such leadership, the culture of an institution becomes increasingly rigid and inwardly focused.

In recent years, I have seen mainline church leaders in every expression of the church change the language of their institutional forms from words such as "division" or "department" or "committee" to words and phrases such as "ministries" or "task forces" or "mission teams." However, a mere adjustment in language seldom has the power to change the fundamental reality and culture of an institution. In the congregation, "mission teams" become just as rigid and self-perpetuating as "functional committees" if they do not include an intentional provision for holding the group accountable to a continually updated vision for the institution as a whole. Likewise, denominational and middle judicatory units and structures become just as rigid and self-perpetuating as "functional committees" if there is no intentional provision for holding the group accountable to a continually updated vision for the institution as a whole.

The further past the peak of the "organizational maturation curve" an institution moves, the more resistant it becomes to such accountabilities and the more difficult it is to begin a "recovery" process. This is due to a number of factors, including increased *anxiety* in the system, momentum (which is the tendency of an object in motion to continue along its current path), and inertia (the tendency of an object at rest to remain at rest).

The organizational maturation curve applies to all expressions of institutional life, and one can easily see the parallel with the "Congregational Life Cycle" (Figure 4-4). Various writers and church organizational specialists have created different versions of the Congregational Life Cycle, but I find George Bullard's version to be the most helpful.[2]

Contextual Obsolescence

If institutions do not adapt to the challenges that current reality presents, they become contextually obsolete and irrelevant. Once a church organization of any expression becomes contextually irrelevant, it begins "slip-sliding away," slipping toward becoming an empty vessel that is no longer of use in God's plans for the transformation of individuals and the world.

Churches become contextually obsolete by losing touch with, and ultimately ceasing to serve, the needs of many or all of the people who live in their mission area. Perhaps the most obvious illustration is the

Fig. 4-4: The Life Cycle of a Congregation © George Bullard

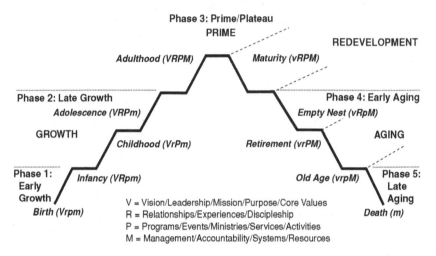

congregation located in a changing neighborhood (of course, *all* neighborhoods are changing *constantly* in various ways). If a congregation becomes overly focused on those who are already members and thus ignores the new people who are moving in, over the course of a few years the congregation may find itself an island in the midst of a sea of racial or ethnic difference.

However, the change in the neighborhood does not have to be as obvious as a complete racial or ethnic change. It may be socioeconomic, age-based, or it may have to do with any number of other more subtle shifts in the population.

The further removed a congregation becomes from the people in its local mission area, the more profound the change that will be required to reconnect and to engage in mission that actually speaks to the needs of the surrounding community.

Generational Obsolescence

Another form of contextual obsolescence that has application in all expressions of church life is generational obsolescence.

Three overarching forms of church organization, or polity, are common among churches today. Each is foreshadowed in the New Testament: the *episcopal* system, which features bishops; the *presbyterian* system, which has a committee (the presbytery) in place of a bishop; and the *congregational* system, which in its purest form grants all authority to the congregation as a whole. There are many variations on these three, but their rudimentary form can be seen in the various mainline denominational systems today.

Each of these three approaches to church organization (episcopal, presbyterian and congregational) has its strengths and weaknesses, its wisdom and its pitfalls. But it is the way these systems adapt from one generation or era to the next that is of particular significance to the discussion here.

The forms of organization and governance currently in use in all eight mainline churches were shaped, or significantly reshaped, in the post-WWII years of the 1940s through the1960s. For example, the United Church of Christ was restructured in 1957 by the merging of four communions, two of which were congregational in polity and two of which were presbyterian in polity. The United Methodist Church was structured in 1968 with the merger of the Methodist Episcopal Church and the Evangelical United Brethren. The Disciples of Christ underwent a significant restructure in 1968. These post–WWII adaptations significantly redefined the role of the denominations and the relationship of congregations to their middle judicatories and the larger denominational bodies.

As important as these formal structural changes were in reshaping the mainline churches, a number of important *informal* structural changes also took place (both formal and informal structural changes are always also *relational* changes). In the case of congregations, perhaps the clearest example is the "functional committee system," introduced in the 1940s and 1950s (and can be found in denominations of all three archetypal polities). I like to call it the "*dysfunctional* committee system" because, in most congregations still using this paradigm, I find that usually less than half of the committees are actually functioning effectively.

While technical adjustments to these forms have been made from time to time during the past forty years, their essence has not changed substantially since the post–WWII era. They emerged to address issues and needs relevant to the WWII generation, based on assumptions that were operative in that era.

For example, the WWII generation loved institutions and institutional life. They flooded into churches, social clubs, and other institutions after the war and, where there were no such institutions, they created them. In contrast, the *post-war* generations have little trust in institutions and little interest in being part of institutional life. Thus organizations that are set up to involve a high percentage of their membership in committee meetings, which the WWII generation enjoyed, are simply obsolete when it comes to addressing the interests of the generations born after 1945. These later generations are interested in *hands-on* mission involvement, but not so much in institutional life per se.

The point here is that since at least 1968, the mainline churches have been functioning in ways that have not been addressing some significant needs and interests of post-war generations. The polity per se is not the problem, it is the way structures are organized *within* the polity that is at issue. The same structural issues are found within all three polities. The WWII generation structured their organizations to reflect their own needs, naturally, not those of the succeeding generations. Thus, much of the restructuring of the mid-1960s was done just in time to be obsolete for younger generations.

How Form Can Undercut Function

We are all familiar with the adage, "form follows function." Well, perhaps form *should* follow function. But in obsolete systems, function has a way of following form. Perhaps the best example can be found in the *hub model* versus the *network model*.

Hubs versus Networks

I have often wondered whether anyone in the Eisenhower administration did a sociological impact study before starting the construction of the interstate highway system. I wonder about this because it had a remarkable impact. For example, consider Route 66, which ran from Los Angeles to Chicago. Not only is most of the road gone, but so are most of the businesses that used to thrive on its steady traffic. Whole towns nearly dried up with the road's demise.

There is no question that the interstate highway is usually the quickest way to travel significant distances (barring a closing due to an accident or road construction). Nevertheless, when I have time, I like to get off the interstate and take an old parallel U.S. highway. I do this for several reasons. For one, there is usually little traffic on the four lanes of a U.S. highway because nearly everyone is over on the interstate. Second, there is often a merciful dearth of fast-food franchises on the U.S. highway, yet still a few mom-and-pop cafes notable for their atmosphere if not for their food. Third, it is a trip down memory lane as you see old tourist camps from the 1930s and truck stops and motels from the 1950s boarded over and abandoned. These once-thriving enterprises went out of business soon after the interstate came in. In some parts of the country, one can also see old road signs for tourist attractions long gone. On old U.S. 19 in northern Florida, "See Webb's City" signs can still be seen, but Webb's closed back in the 1970s.

It isn't that I am anti–interstate highways. When I was the Disciples' regional minister for Tennessee, I drove I-40 from Memphis to Knoxville, I-24 from Clarksville to Chattanooga, and I-71 from Knoxville to the Tri-cities in a state that is some 600 miles long from the southwest to the northeast corner. Driving along at high speed, measuring my progress from one public radio station to the next, I often wondered about my predecessors who had to cover that ground on old federal and state highways. I frequently drove from Nashville to Memphis in the morning (three hours), went to meetings all day and evening, and then drove home, arriving by 1:00 a.m. to sleep in my own bed. Years ago the trip would have taken more than twice as long. But consider *East* Tennessee. It is beautiful mountainous country. The old "state secretaries" (the predecessors to regional ministers) must have left home for days or weeks at a time in order to make driving all those miles of twisting turning roads as productive as possible. In many ways, the interstates are a blessing.

However, they were not always a blessing to those who lived near where they were built. They brought profound change to nearly every aspect of life. In the 1950s, much of North America looked like the illustration below.

Fig. 4-5: Small Town America before the Interstates

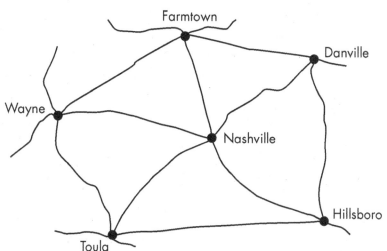

Small and medium-sized towns, each linked by roads, comprised much of the countryside. Town folk often knew a number of people in neighboring towns because their high school teams played each other and their churches had fifth Sunday night meetings. Each town had their own social and economic infrastructure with small businesses and social clubs. Everybody knew everybody. Many families lived in these towns for generations. However, the interstate highways changed this picture profoundly.

Many of the roads that had connected each of these towns to the others were cut off by the interstate. One can see some of these formerly vital links dead-ending at the chain link fence of the interstate right-of-way. Some of these old roads were routed over the interstates via bridges, but sociologists soon discovered that overpasses are psychological

Fig. 4-6: The Highway Comes in

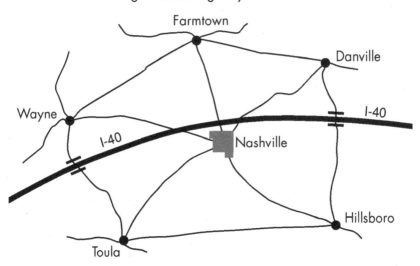

barriers to most of us. They feel like, and effectively become, a boundary of sorts.

The town that happens to be near the interstate becomes the site for on-off ramps, which often leads to a scenario similar to the following: The interstate exits become a beehive of economic activity. First a gas station or two appear, then a restaurant and a motel, then another gas station and another motel, and a fast-food chain or two. Then a truck stop comes, and a small commercial center. Gradually (or sometimes remarkably quickly), these towns with the on-off ramps become hubs of economic activity. Not only do the on-off ramps attract business from those passing by on the interstate, but those who live in small towns nearby have to go to the town with the on-off ramps to get onto the interstate. If someone in a neighboring small town wants to get to another small town in the area, they often have to go through the town with an on-off ramp to find a road that will get them there, or they may go to one interstate entrance and travel an exit or two before getting off to travel a secondary road to their destination. All of this means increasing economic activity in the towns with the on-off ramps. Small to medium-sized shopping malls have developed in many of these places, followed by box stores like Wal-Mart.

While the towns on the interstate are growing, the economic activity in the surrounding small towns begins to shrink as people find they can drive to the growing "hub" towns and find more commercial choices and lower prices. Young people, following jobs, begin leaving the small towns for the new economic centers. Soon the local schools begin to shrink and then to give way to consolidations that create new regional schools, usually located not far from an on-off ramp of the highway. Many of the small towns shrink away until there are only houses occupied mostly by elderly persons and a downtown row of empty shops (although most still have a pizza shop and a gas station that rents videos...sometimes these are the same establishment). And there are usually several small struggling churches, whose congregations wonder what happened to the "good old days" when the church house was nearly full every Sunday.

Though it used to be that lots of the members of a church in one town knew lots of members in the churches of the same denomination in the surrounding towns, now only one or two members know one or two in the others. Perhaps they met them at an area or state denominational event, being among the few to attend. Now many of the members of a congregation in one town are not even aware that the congregation with a similar name in the next town is of the same denominational family.

What I have just described is not only the pattern of towns in the wake of interstate highway construction. It is also the pattern seen in congregations that operate in a pastor-centered style (the pastor is the hub town with the interstate connection). It is also the pattern in most middle judicatories and denominational units, as these have increasingly become hubs of control and communication. The flow of communication and relationship in these congregations has ceased to be from congregation to congregation and has become "congregation to middle judicatory and back," with occasional "congregation to denominational unit and back."

This phenomenon is nowhere more pronounced among mainline churches than in the Disciples of Christ, which moved from being a convention of congregations to a denomination in 1968. It is no coincidence that the Disciples' Restructure process, which was a centralizing process and which created middle judicatories (regions) as we know them today, occurred in 1968—just at the height of interstate highway construction. Many mainline middle judicatory executives are the center of regional ecclesial life and hence become something of a hindrance to the work because more needs to happen than can squeeze through the pastoral, programmatic, and administrative "pipeline" of a middle judicatory executive. Thus, "ministry capacity" effectively shrinks.

But this phenomenon also mirrors pastor-centered styles of congregational ministry (as defined by Arlin Rothauge) so common among mainline congregations across the country.[3] A "pastor-centered" church is one in which, as the description implies, everything that happens in the life of the institution must be approved, touched, or facilitated by the pastor. These congregations usually have participating memberships of between seventy-five and five hundred. These congregations seldom

Fig. 4-7: The Middle Judicatory Becomes a Hub

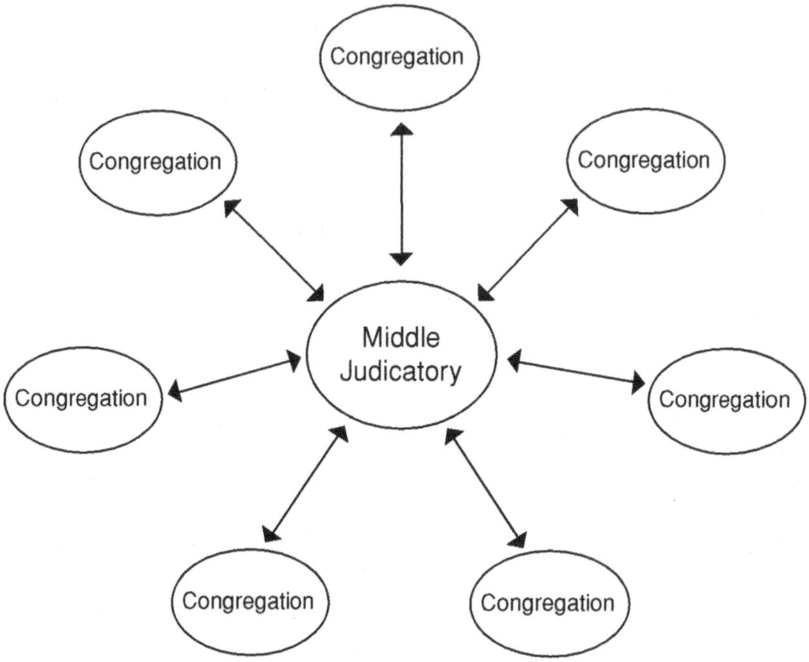

have more than five hundred members because the pastor-centered model limits how much activity and creativity can occur in a congregation, since the pastor can touch only so much.

To be sure, other events and trends were contemporaneous with the interstate highway system and helped to bring about this phenomenon of hubs replacing networks. In many ways, this describes the logical and inevitable conclusion of the entire modern era. Farming moved to a larger scale, using larger and more sophisticated machines, which meant fewer farm jobs; small businesses were swept up in corporate mergers; electrical power came to be increasingly centralized; huge telecommunication firms bought up local telephone companies; and so forth.

The point here is that the structure and day-to-day functioning of our mainline denominational structures is modern in character and cannot meet the needs of members, ministers, and congregations. This is especially true as middle judicatory and denominational unit staffs have shrunk in the face of financial cutbacks, and as increasing demands have been placed on congregational ministers.

A new kind of "*networking*" model is needed in all expressions. In denominational units, this means forsaking the "panel of experts" model in which "one size fits all" programs are developed and pressed onto congregations. An effective denominational unit today will network and broker resources both inside and outside of the unit and the denomination. Frankly, because most denominational units have not been doing this, congregations of all denominations have been tapping into extra-denominational networks on their own. One of the worst-kept secrets in mainline denominations is how many congregational ministers seek the help they need from wherever they can find it, including from sources that might not be "approved" by denominational executives, when they can't get it through the denomination itself.

In middle judicatories, this means networking congregations that have certain resources with those congregations that need the resources; networking ministers and lay leaders with those in other congregations within the middle judicatory; finding ways to encourage, equip, and empower leaders rather than focusing so much on regulation and control. Holding ministers, members, and congregations accountable is an important function of judicatories, but there is a difference between "holding accountable" and "over-controlling."

In congregations, it means the pastor leads the congregation in a way that helps laypeople identify their own gifts for ministry and that helps equip, empower, and hold them accountable for ministry. It is worth noting that in Ephesians 4, ministers are called to "equip" the saints, not to *be the saint.*

That brings us to the third element of the "perfect storm" confronting the mainline churches: *anxiety.*

The Third Element of the Perfect Storm

The "High Pressure" of Anxiety

The "Perfect Storm" that has confronted the mainline church in recent decades represents the collision of several elements including: the dramatic shift of American culture from the modern into the postmodern era, the increasingly obsolete organizational forms inherited from the modern era, and the fear that has turned us inward toward maintenance and survival rather than mission.

We live in a culture of high anxiety. Anxiety is in the very air we breathe in North America. As a culture built on risk (entrepreneurialism), we have always been an anxious people. We turned Pearl Harbor into a cultural icon of unease and the need to be constantly "vigilant." The Cold War featured bombers, submarines, and intercontinental ballistic missiles on hair-trigger alert, bringing the constant threat of nuclear annihilation. The threats from other governments were overshadowed by a new kind of threat on September 11, 2001. It is difficult to overestimate the impact of the events of that day.

For many decades, the United States had enjoyed the "protection" of two oceans and friendly borders to the north and south. Since the War Between the States, our wars have always been fought on someone else's landscape. Thus, what had been practically unthinkable, an enemy attack on U.S. soil, became reality. Seared into the American psyche were the images of the airliners being flown into the World Trade Center

Towers, the crater left by United Flight 93 in the Pennsylvania country-side, and the smoldering breach in the walls of the Pentagon.

In the wake of 9/11, the government instituted an alert system with various levels of "alert status" indicated by colors. The years since 9/11 have seen the United States constantly under "alert," from at least "yellow" up to "orange." Though the government has raised the level of alert numerous times over the years Homeland Security has usually been unable or unwilling to pinpoint a particular threat. The practical effect has been little except to further raise people's anxiety. Also, we hear that our airports are still unsafe and that nuclear material may be coming into our country through our seaports.

Americans understand quite well the hostile relationships with foreign *governments*. That has been a hallmark of the modern era: nation vying against nation. What has made our anxiety more intense is that this new enemy is *not* a government. It is a shadowy, underground *movement* of people who are using our own technologies against us. The tactics and many of the weapons we have brought with us from the Cold War into the postmodern era don't seem to be very effective against such an enemy.

In such a time of high anxiety, we naturally want to *do* something. This may explain why so many Americans—from the White House, to Congress, to the general public—were willing to enter into war with Iraq.

It is now clear that there was no real evidence to back claims of weapons of mass destruction in Iraq and no material threat to the United States and its allies. But we, as a people, have only ourselves and our own anxiety to blame for allowing our government (both Republicans and Democrats) to rush into a war that was fundamentally unrelated to September 11; a war with no exit strategy; a war that failed to address the political realities of that region and the world; a war that seemed to forget all the lessons of American involvement in Vietnam; a war that has generated more terrorists than have been killed or captured.

Inevitably, we are reacting to the war in Iraq, fearful that we have once again gotten ourselves into a quagmire, and are without a clue as to how to extricate ourselves responsibly. Liberals and conservatives alike look for places to lay blame, and everyone is uneasy.

In the meantime, China and India are rising as economic competitors and as competitors for oil. We see jobs going overseas. We see scandals that challenge our assumptions about the integrity of our corporate leaders and the viability of our business institutions. We worry about the cost of health care and whether we will be able to afford or even get health insurance. We see what looks to us like astronomical fuel prices. We are now, finally, accepting the reality of global warming.

Add to this list that, even before 9/11, few of us understood the shift from the "modern" world to the "postmodern," which began in earnest around 1968 and which continues unabated to this day. Most of us are holding on to our *modern* socioeconomic and political understandings: understandings based on a world order that was driven by the sovereignty of nation-states, from the sixteenth century well into the twentieth. We have not understood that the world order is now based on global markets and mass communication as much as upon nation-states. Global markets transcend national boundaries, communication satellites perceive no national boundaries from space, and nation-states can do little to regulate or control them. These are fundamental issues of the *postmodern* world.[1]

In our anxiety, we crave certainty. Both liberals and conservatives tend to become more fundamentalist and their voices more shrill. That is, both liberals and conservatives appeal to bedrock assumptions that, typical of modern paradigms, do not change, are absolute, and *no longer function effectively.*

Add to these political and economic realities that our consumer culture has been built on the denial of death and the worship of youth. We are encouraged to believe that if only we buy the right products, we will be forever young. It has been said that Baby Boomers are the first generation to believe that death is *optional.* Yet at some deeper level we know better. And it makes us nervous.

In the midst of all this anxiety in the culture at large, we see that our beloved mainline church institutions are declining in both numbers and power. Yet ironically, because of our anxieties, we do not want our institutions to change.

Anyone who has tried to lead in a system that needs to change, and yet is resistant to change, knows that it is a tough place to live. An institution, or any expression of it, that has slipped down the slope of decline (the right half of the "organizational maturation curve") and is resistant to the very change that it needs becomes anxious, compulsive, and fearful. On some level, most of the leaders and members *know* that change is needed, but they *hate and fear* it. So they resist needed change. They resist it by engaging in denial, changing the subject, and blocking any effort to effect deeper change.

Leaders, and especially the primary staff person or persons, usually bear the brunt of this behavior, becoming targets and scapegoats. This is especially true when they try to help the institution cut through the denial and act in spite of anxieties. This is one key to the high rate of "burnout" we see among so many ministers these days (and among the leaders of so many other institutions). Some individuals act out their fears through the system and the system acts out fears through individuals.[2]

Beyond garden variety anxieties, individuals who have real, deep spiritual and emotional pathologies often find an anxious system a very welcoming place for them to act out their un-health. Again, leaders are most often the targets of these behaviors. They have been called "clergy killers," among other things.[3] If unchecked, they are also church killers.

Though the problems of an organization will often be blamed on the immediately previous leader (sometimes by the *current* anxious leader), most systems in crisis have been in trouble for some time. The last leader may or may not have effectively addressed the issues, but the issues faced by mainline churches can seldom be "cured" in one seven- to- ten-year term of leadership and the problems are seldom *due* simply to one term of leadership.

In the face of these dynamics, Edwin Friedman described effective leaders as a "non-anxious presence."[4] That is, leaders need to maintain a healthy distance from what is happening in the system while yet being emotionally invested and present to people. But every leader who has been under fire knows that it is easy to lose one's objectivity and, while being physically present, to become emotionally absent. Thus, instead of being a non-anxious presence, it is easy to become an anxious non-presence.

Unhealthy elements in a system will always seek to "hook" unhealthy elements within the leader. Even the healthiest leader will find an anxious system to be a formidable place to live and work. She or he had better take care of her/his own spiritual, emotional, and physical needs, drawing regularly from the deep wells of the Spirit's presence and power.

Creating a Holding Environment

Ron Heifetz, who gives us the distinction between "technical change" and "adaptive change," draws on the discipline of psychology for the term "holding environment."[5] When change is needed, it is a function of leadership to create a "holding environment" in which constructive change can happen. Heifetz uses the image of a "pressure cooker" to illustrate.

A pressure cooker is a large pan with a lid that seals airtight. Built into the lid is a steam valve. A measure of water is put into the pan along with the food to be cooked. When the lid is secured and the heat is applied, steam develops and raises the pressure in the pan and the food begins to cook.

When the cooking pressure is just right, the steam valve on the lid rattles intermittently. If the steam valve isn't rattling, there is not enough heat being applied and nothing is cooking. On the other hand, if the steam valve is rattling constantly, one must either turn down the heat a bit or step back...because dinner is about to be spewed onto the ceiling!

It is in the balance between "not enough heat" and "too much heat" that there exists a holding environment in which cooking can occur.

Adaptive change creates heat and pressure of another kind in an organization. This is the emotional heat and pressure generated by the experience of loss itself and by the fear of loss. Though the underlying feelings are those of grief and fear, these will most often surface in various expressions of *anger.* Why is anger often the emotion of choice? Perhaps because anger feels powerful, while fear makes one feel powerless and vulnerable, and no one much likes feeling powerless and vulnerable. (Why else are so many people given to "road rage" in a time of high anxiety?)

The "trick" for leaders is to keep enough heat on so that something is cooking, but not to raise the temperature so high that there will be an explosion and a mess. This means the leader must be able to tolerate a certain level of discomfort in the body, which is not easy for the many ministers who are sensitive to feelings both naturally and by training. It is especially difficult for ministers and other leaders who are "people pleasers" by nature.

While some people have a rather high tolerance for heat, some others have practically no tolerance for heat and will begin whining and acting out the instant it is even *suggested* that something might be about to change. Nevertheless, those quickest to feel the slightest heat must not be allowed to set the agenda and pace of change, for they will stymie change altogether.

Too little heat and a congregation (or other expression of the church) will become passive and unchanging. Too much heat and a congregation (or other expression of the church) will become agitated to the point of breaking down and, most often, lashing out (member against member, member against leader, even leader against leader).

Thus, the kind of leadership that pushes an organization toward deeper and more significant adaptive change is not only often *uncomfortable,* it is also inherently *risky.* It is risky to operate within the "uncomfortably hot but not catastrophically hot" zone. However, it is also risky *not* to push. "Leaders" who allow the pot to grow cold will find resentment among members who, even though not comfortable with change, know that change needs to occur or else the death of their beloved institution will be imminent. As the institution slides further and further into decline, leaders will find themselves increasingly subject to passive-aggressive "acting out" of grief and fear by members looking for targets of blame.

The demands of leadership in such a context of "high anxiety" are enormous. There are the daily demands of an anxious system and there are the larger and longer-term responsibilities of bringing the system itself to some measure of health and effectiveness. This means one must not allow oneself to be drawn into the anxiety and dis-ease of the system. But how does one stay differentiated? My experience suggests that leaders must daily keep three questions before themselves.

The Three Most Important Questions

The first question is, *"What time is it?"*

As internal and external circumstances change over time, systems must respond with appropriate change in order to remain healthy and effective. However, because anxiety-laden systems love homeostasis even more than health, the members of declining institutions are encouraged to engage in denial. This means that in mainline denominations, and in most of their static or declining component organizations, the institutional culture will do its best to convince everyone, including the leaders, that it is 1955. It is *not* 1955, 1965, nor even 1995. Thus, leaders must constantly ask, "What time is it *now?*"

The second question is, *"Where am I?"*

Institutional culture will most often try to convince everyone, including the leaders, that the institution is situated in a place that no longer exists. It is likely a "place" where little change is needed, a place where the mission is nonthreatening and crystal clear: *do more of the same only do it harder and faster!*

If you are in a static or declining denominational agency or structure, this means institutional culture will try to convince you that the headquarters building *is* the definitive place of reality and that anyplace else, where things appear to be different, is really just an anomaly. If you are in a static or declining congregation, this means the institutional culture will try to convince you that the congregation is situated in a neighborhood that remains friendly to the congregation as it is, a neighborhood that needs exactly what the congregation is offering, a neighborhood in which the residents look and act much like those who lived there when many of the current members of the congregation became members, a neighborhood full of people that would want to become a part of the congregation "if we could just get the word out and let people know we are here."

The reality is that ecclesial, national, and global realities change in significant ways over time, and denominational leadership must effectively respond to the new realities or risk obsolescence. Likewise, neighborhoods change demographically and in other ways over time (and not much time at that) and congregations must change in response or risk becoming contextually obsolete and irrelevant.

The third question is, *"What am I doing here?"*

This may be the most important question of all in an institutional context (local or denominational) where so many people are dedicated to their own agendas or are being "used" by the system to distract faithful and effective leaders from the needed agenda. Leaders must constantly ask questions such as: "What did God call me here to do?" "What did the church call me here to do?" "How does what I am doing *today* fit with my overall purpose and objectives as a leader?"

These questions are so important because institutional culture is so powerful and if we are not consciously thinking about these things, we will be swept along by the currents of the system's own *hubris*. This means we will be doing technical change, even though we *think* we are doing adaptive change.

PART II

Challenges Confronting Mainline Churches Today

In Part 1, we reviewed three elements of a "perfect storm" that has led to the current crises in mainline church life.

First, a "hurricane of change" in American culture has driven the mainline churches from a place of cultural privilege and dominance to the margins of society. The culture no longer carries the language and concepts of Christian faith for the mainline church. As American culture has become increasingly secular, society has become less and less interested in what the mainline churches think or say. When the culture *does* want a religious perspective, it is the fundamentalist right-wing churches that most often get the attention of the media. This is a phenomenon that increasingly is as much a concern to moderately conservative churches as to mainline churches. The media showcases fundamentalism because it speaks in absolutes, in straightforward statements that are well suited to sound "bytes." Real engagement of spiritual issues does not fit into a two-minute time slot or a 10-inch newshole.

Second, in many cases the mainline denominations, in all their expressions, are still using organizational forms and approaches that were created in the post–WWII era or before, which are thus obsolete in the postmodern era. Yet, in spite of the need for organizational reform, entrenched bureaucracies in congregations, middle judicatories, and denominational units tend to focus on the needs of the system itself and thus make needed change difficult.

Third, the anxiety that has developed in the mainline church and its component institutions in the face of the shrinkage of membership and resources tends to shift the attention of the organization from the *mission* of the church to the *survival* of the church. Said another way, *survival becomes the mission,* and thus decline is further hastened.

With these three elements in mind, let's look more closely at some of the challenges confronting the mainline churches today.

6

Generational Differences

In order to lead effectively in the church today, it is essential to understand that this is the first time in its two thousand year history that the church has had to minister to five or more generations simultaneously.

Biologically, a "generation" is usually described as about twenty years in length. On average, people are living much longer these days, so there are significant numbers of people of older generations living today. However, perhaps even more significant is the sociological or cultural sense of the term "generation." That is, people born in the same era generally share key sociological traits and perspectives. Sociologically, then, a generation is a group of people who share the same formative experiences and, thus, whose worldview is much the same.

Through much of human history, major cultural shifts often lasted hundreds of years. However, the world is moving so rapidly today that less than twenty years can create huge differences in how the world operates and how it is experienced by contemporaries.

Thus, by both the biological and sociological definitions, we have several distinctly different generations currently living. The differences between these generations are not simply "psycho-socially developmental" in nature (though we know that people do tend to see things differently at different times in the human life cycle). These cohorts are also profoundly different from those of other generations because of the life-shaping experiences they hold in common.

Various researchers use somewhat different frameworks and names for these groupings. But they are generally quite similar. For example, in many of his writings George Barna refers to the WWII generation as "Builders," while some other researchers refer to them as "Boosters."

These groups can be identified as follows: the Depression Era generation (born before 1915), the WWII generation (born 1915–1930), the Silent generation (born 1931–1944), the early Baby Boomer generation (born 1945-1955), the late Baby Boomer generation (born 1956–1965), Baby Busters (called Generation X by some researchers, born 1966–1982), and Millennials (called Generation Y or Next by some researchers, born since 1982). Of course, some individuals will better "fit" with a generation before or after them, but these general groupings are remarkably useful because they identify traits common to so many who share the same birth interval. Most people find they "fit" their generational description in important ways. The members of each group have distinctive ways of looking at the world because of the events that were occurring during the time they were growing up. For example:

- The Depression Era generation (born before 1915) was shaped by their experience of the Depression with its shortages and limitations. These folks tend to be cautious, appreciative of structure, and somewhat suspicious of institutions (they remember when the banks failed). They save things most of us throw away without a thought. There are relatively few of this generation still with us, but most mainline congregations have some, though they may have limited mobility.
- The WWII generation (born 1915–1930) was shaped by their experience of that war. They have a strong sense of duty and loyalty to persons and institutions. They "saved the world" by getting organized and have been organizers and institution builders ever since.
- The Silent generation (born 1931–1944) was too young to serve in World War II, but they were deeply influenced by it as they were entering adulthood. The Korean War was theirs to fight, but unlike WWII, it was described as a "police action" and was more ambiguous in its goals. Small in numbers and in some ways overshadowed by the WWII generation, they have produced many effective managers but not as many visionary leaders.
- The Baby Boomer generation (born 1945–1965) was born and raised during a time of unparalleled economic expansion and optimism. They were told they could do and be anything they wanted, and many of them believed it. Nevertheless, they were deeply disillusioned by their experience of the Vietnam War and the bigotry exposed by the civil rights movement. Thus, they do not easily trust government or other institutions generally.

- Baby Busters (or Generation X, as some sociologists prefer, born 1965 to 1982), grew up in times of shortages and lowered expectations and so they tend to be more conservative (some economically, some socially, some both) in outlook than their Boomer parents. Many of them were raised in single-parent or two-working-parents homes and were thus parented as much or more by peers as by their parents. They place a high value on community and are concerned about various social issues, but have little loyalty to institutions. Though initially pegged as "slackers," this generation has turned out to have a fairly strong work ethic. They take parenting quite seriously, perhaps in reaction to their own childhood experiences.
- Millennials (or Generation Y or Next, as some prefer, born 1982–2000), are still quite young, and so it is difficult to say exactly how they will develop. However, they have been raised with computers, and many spend a great deal of time in the "virtual" world, relating through e-mail. Their experience includes instantaneous information, which they can easily access and pass through the Internet. This seems to have given them a confidence in their ability to "change the world." Fads and cultural idioms come and go among Millennials at incredible speed because, again, they are connected through the Internet.

This represents the barest outline of these various peer groups. Each generation has its own distinctive attitudes regarding spirituality and worship styles, and approaches to education, money, institutions, and most everything else one can name. Of course, there are cohorts of every generation who more closely resemble those of the previous or succeeding generations, so one must not be rigid in the application of these generational groupings. Each generation has its own strengths, weaknesses, and temptations. I personally reject the often-expressed sentiment that one generation is better than another. Each generation is different and distinct and has both its good and bad characteristics.

Below we will look somewhat more in depth at the experience of the WWII generation and the Baby Boomers. This is because the mainline church today was significantly shaped and reshaped by the World War II generation and most of the primary leaders of the mainline churches today are Baby Boomers. Also, their legacy confronts those of younger generations who are now coming to leadership (Busters and Millennials).

"The Greatest Generation"

Tom Brokaw's books depicting and describing the generation that fought WWII as "The Greatest Generation" struck a chord in the American psyche and became runaway best-sellers. Part of the appeal, no doubt, had to do with the ambiguity of our times today. In the WWII era, at least in retrospect, there seemed to be a kind of moral clarity, a clear line of demarcation between evil and good.

Of course, compared to the perpetrators of the Holocaust and the Massacre of Nanjing, the Allies *did* look righteous. But that righteousness was, of course, only relative. For example, we Americans had our own mass exterminations on the American frontier a century earlier, and our nation participated heartily in slavery and in its benefits to the privileged. Colonialism perpetrated by the nations of the North (including the United States) was the order of the day in most of the Southern Hemisphere, and neocolonialism is still with us. But of course, the human condition is such that whenever victors look back on history, they see themselves as more virtuous than they really were (which means, of course, that most of us reading this book see ourselves as more virtuous than we really are).

Brokaw's books also appealed because the American WWII generation understood itself as having "saved the world." Again, there is a sense in which this claim is justifiable. Hitler, Tojo, and Mussolini were no small threats to the world. On the other hand, in regard to the G.I. generation of the United States having "saved the world," it must be admitted that the British held off the Germans for a long time before America entered the war. The Soviets stopped Hitler on the Eastern front at an incredibly high price (tens of millions of casualties). And the Chinese and other Asian peoples sacrificed immensely in resisting the Empire of Japan.[1]

While a huge factor in the Allies' victory was the ability of the United States, and of the Soviet Union, to outproduce Germany and Japan, the confident spirit of the American soldier was also a major factor in victory. No doubt, many factors contributed to this spirit. But one significant factor was the notion that God was acting in the world through the United States and its allies on behalf of truth and justice. How could they lose? These essentially theological notions, America as a morally superior nation and as an intentional instrument of God, were both inherited from early American tradition and carefully cultivated by American political and religious leadership.

The confidence of the American soldier in WWII can also be attributed in part to the modern notion, so much at the heart of the American experience and self-image, that progress was inevitable and that the world could be *organized* into perfection or, if you will, organized into the "kingdom of God." The excesses of Hitler and the Axis were understood at a deep level to be the last gasps of chaos struggling against the inevitable victory of divine order. This was "modernism" at its logical conclusion and at its most naïve.

Thus, when the war was over, many felt at a very deep yet unconscious level that the kingdom of Heaven was at hand, and people set about creating the kind of organizations and institutions that would establish and maintain God's order. In that spirit, congregations and mainline denominational structures were significantly reshaped (within the boundaries of basic polity). Thus, for example, mainline congregations and denominations and other mainline organizations across the United States implemented the "functional committee system," which is a product of modern organizational thinking. Mainline denominational structures themselves were significantly reshaped in the mid-1940s through the late 1960s in a way that reflected this trust in "organization as savior."

Since there was an underlying "modern" assumption in this "era of restructuring" that they could, and were, getting the engineering "right," *the new organizations were not created to foster and nurture ongoing change within them.* They were created to be self-perpetuating and to *resist* change. The significance of this statement for church leadership cannot be overstated. It means that, rather than being seen as a means to an end (a tool of mission), there is a real sense in which the organizations came to be seen as ends in themselves. These organizations were thought to embody the power to transform the world. Thus, the purpose of leadership was not so much to call and lead the organization to constant reform, but to *maintain* the organization and make sure that it all ran according to plan. The purpose and design for leadership, then, was primarily bureaucratic and became focused on management and maintenance. Innovation would be prized only insofar as it was directed toward maintenance of the organizational status quo, not if its aim was fundamental change of the organization itself. The organization was perceived primarily as an agent of change in the world, not as subject to the need for change itself.

This was a case in which the "modern" assumption that evil could be organized out of the world was at odds with the traditional Protestant theological assumption that, while humans have a responsibility to change the world, the instruments (including organizations) created to change the world are as subject to the human condition as is the world itself. Thus, John Calvin and other Protestant thinkers would say, the world can never be changed once and for all until the close of the age, and then by divine intervention only.

In a sense, then, the WWII generation was both the logical conclusion and an incarnation of the "modern" era. On the one hand, it must be admitted that it *was* a "great" generation. It demonstrated great courage and strength in the face of tremendous adversity and threat. I, for one, would not want to live under the likes of Nazis and warlords. On the other hand, it was possessed by a kind of theological naiveté and social and political arrogance for which the world is still paying today. It was (and remains) so powerful that to this day, we still see the U.S.

government trying to export American *forms* in the uncritical belief that these socioeconomic-political forms are superior to all others in bringing about justice and that America always knows best what constitutes justice itself.

It is not my intention to impugn the motives of the individual members of the WWII generation (which included my own parents). In the end, I believe it must again be admitted that every generation has its strengths and its weaknesses and is shaped by its own times. But it must also be admitted that succeeding generations should always be careful about uncritically accepting their predecessors' assumptions, as did so many of the Silent generation (born 1930–1945) and not a few of the Baby Boomer generation as well (born 1945–65).

The WWII generation lived out a very powerful cultural myth that created and reshaped organizational structures in the 1940s and beyond. But while these organizational structures worked for the most part until 1968, they are highly resistant to change and reform even in the face of apparent and overwhelming evidence that they are no longer functioning effectively. Leaders who set out to reform such structures will not only be encountering the normal resistance that is inherent to *every* human form, but also risk being misunderstood at least and, at worst, demonized, because they are "messing" with powerful cultural paradigms that are deeply rooted in the American psyche.

The "Mainline" Mind-set

The WWII generation loved institutions, and why wouldn't they? Part of the experience of living during the Second World War was being caught up in institutions that addressed critical issues and that prescribed how daily life would be lived. Whether serving in the military, or in a production facility, or simply living the life of any ordinary citizen, institutions (military, industrial, governmental, and social) shaped much of daily life.

This is not to say, exactly, that soldiers loved the military. But like all soldiers in every era, though they may hate the army, they are indelibly shaped by the experience. As a young pastor, I remember seeing deacons (responsible in my tradition for collecting the offering and distributing communion during corporate worship) who were veterans of WWII standing at the communion table waiting to receive the trays. They stood at "parade rest" until receiving their trays and then shifted to "attention" before marching off the chancel and on to the rows of pews.

A portion of the WWII experience that was so powerful was in being a part of something larger than oneself. In 1940, the United States was still a largely agrarian nation of small towns and rural areas. The disillusionment caused by WWI and the Great Depression of the 1930s had created an American attitude of isolationism toward the world and isolated living in daily life. Much of the population focused on survival. So when the call went out after Pearl Harbor for recruits for armed forces and factories, it resulted in what was for many a new experience of being "part of something larger." People from the rural South were thrown together with people from Midwestern small towns and from large cities of the Northeast. It was exciting and, while at first *dis*-orienting, it was ultimately *re*-orienting.

By the time the war was over, that generation had been reshaped forever. As much as they might have complained about the military or the factory, after the war they built up social organizations in much the same image. The people of the WWII generation were "joiners." They joined lodges and clubs and churches. And when they moved to the newly created suburbs where there were no lodges and clubs and churches, they *created* them. They found meaning in being a part of these institutions. It was an extension of their experience of being caught up in "something larger than themselves."

While I do not wish to overstate the point here, there is a sense in which *the institution itself became the bearer of salvation.*

I am reminded of a conversation with one church leader who was reacting to the damage he perceived a certain ultra-conservative political-action group was causing to our denomination. He said, "I am one of those people who wasn't saved by Jesus. I was saved by the church! And it makes me angry when anyone does damage to the church!"

One often experiences an implicit belief in older members of congregations that are near closing: "If my church dies before I do, I won't get to heaven!"

Some folks were able to put the lodge and the club in *place* of the church. These three institutions were, for them, practically interchangeable because the point was to be a part of something larger, something that would be an "organizing center" of one's life. Many of these same folks had a similar kind of relationship with the companies for which they worked, a relationship so powerful that retirement would prove to be immediately fatal for many.

They sincerely and enthusiastically put their time and money where their hearts were. To this day, most of the church's missions, ministries, and institutions (including congregations, denominational structures, colleges, and seminaries) are drawing on the financial commitments of the WWII generation.

Contrast these shaping experiences of the WWII generation with those of the Baby Boomers.

The Baby Boomer Experience

In contrast to the WWII generation, it is hard to imagine a shaping experience more different than that of the Baby Boomers. The experience of a war shaped both generations, but there the similarities end. If WWII was perceived to be unambiguous in its purpose and its moral rightness, the Vietnam War was exactly the opposite. The Secretary of Defense during most of the war was Robert S. McNamara. He published a book thirty years later that confirmed what many Baby Boomers had long suspected: there was no clear purpose for the war.[2] American involvement in Vietnam began with the Eisenhower and Kennedy administrations, but grew enormously with the Johnson administration. The Johnson and Nixon administrations simply could find no way for the United States to withdraw without losing face.

Thus, some 58,000 Americans and untold numbers of Asians were killed in a war without a clear purpose. The height of the war, 1965–1973, came just as so many early Baby Boomers reached draft age. In the end, whether one fought in the war or in one way or another avoided fighting in the war, most Baby Boomers felt betrayed by their country. Though many mainline *denominational* leaders were beginning to speak out against the war to various degrees by 1968, congregations mostly supported mainline culture and the continuing WWII ethos by encouraging young men to "do their duty," or, at most, congregations kept silent on the matter. These same mainline congregations were also bastions of the culture's racism. Thus, Baby Boomers experienced these churches as part of the problem rather than part of the solution.

I believe that those of us who are "mainline" Baby Boomers must admit that as a generation we were in many ways a pretty selfish lot. If our parents were into "being a part of institutions," we were into radical individualism and "entitlement." While many of us as youth enjoyed singing folk songs about peace and justice, few of us were actually willing to do anything about it. Many of us have enjoyed an unprecedented prosperity made possible by our parents, but we have mostly used it to indulge ourselves. When one looks back at the lyrics of so much of the protest music of the 1960s, one wonders how so many of us came to live such exploitative and environmentally polluting lifestyles today. Our experiences undercut what we had been taught about the world, and we seem to have parlayed our youthful disillusionment into a generational binge.

Hence, our distaste for institutions generally, and religious institutions in particular, is due to a combination of factors: (1) legitimate disillusionment with "modern" institutions that were not up to the challenges of the world they helped to create, and (2) hedonistic rejection of anything that might place restraints on our personal freedom (including, some would say, the bonds of marriage and the legitimate responsibilities of parenting).

Our children have typically responded by looking to small groups of friends for the companionship and intimacy they seldom received at home, and by looking for ways to effectively contribute to the alleviation of suffering in the world. However, the church is not a place most of them look to find such ways to contribute because few of them have ever been associated with a church in any meaningful way. For many, their only experience of "church" is what they have seen on television (Falwell, the Bakers, Robertson, Swaggart, etc.). They have a sense of spirituality, but organized religion is not how they typically express that spirituality.

So while *some* Baby Boomers have returned to the mainline churches of their childhood, few of our congregations have significant numbers of Baby Busters or Millennials. But even the relatively small remnant of Baby Boomer church members find mainline church life to be frustrating because so many of our congregations are still operating on the basis of the same organizational forms that were shaped by the WWII generation.

Even congregations that are now being led by Baby Boomers have trouble appealing to subsequent generations because, frankly speaking as a Baby Boomer myself, we still have a tendency to see the church as existing for the sake of our own needs only and, more painfully, because we still do not know and understand our own children and their needs.

Through most of the last half of the twentieth century, the power of the WWII generation led to a kind of moral and institutional arrogance that insisted they had *the* "Truth," and that younger generations should meet them where they were. Thus, "evangelism" was a matter of keeping the church building open and in good repair and of providing a smiling greeter to meet those unchurched who would be coming to visit. Because the institution itself came to be the means of salvation, "church growth" and "evangelism" were seen as the same thing. In many ways, these churches that were dominated by the WWII generation came to be representative of modern mainline culture itself (which, whatever good qualities it represented, also tended to be a mix of nationalism, racism, and narrow moralism) and were thus increasingly the focus of the angst and anger of younger generations.

To this day, most WWII–generation church members have little clue why their children (and their children's children) are alienated from the mainline churches and see them as mostly irrelevant to their lives and spirituality. Those Baby Boomers who stayed with the church, or have returned, have little more understanding of their children's spiritual needs than did their own parents.

I often ask church groups the following question: "If you were going to start a mission in the Congo, what is the first thing you would do?" Usually the answer comes back, "Learn the language." I go on to say, "Exactly! You would learn French, the universal language of the Congo, and then, as soon as possible, you would seek to learn the local African dialects so you could understand and communicate most effectively."

In this era, our five or six generations don't know much about who each other are. We don't "speak each other's language," or understand what brings each other joy or pain. We are native to our *own* generation's perspective and all others are foreigners to us.

Postmodern society, with its capacity for creating "cultural niches," makes it possible for these generations to each live in its own little world without much real encounter with the others. Each generation has TV shows, music, movies. and radio stations targeted to it. Each has magazines, cruise lines, automobiles, whole neighborhoods, and churches targeted to it.

If we Christians who are members of the WWII and Baby Boomer generations are going to try to reach out to subsequent generations with the gospel, we must learn their language and culture. We must learn who they are and seek to meet them where they are.

We usually think of mentors as older people with wisdom born of experience, who share that wisdom with younger people. Such mentoring is important, and there needs to be more of it happening. However, in the face of the rapid change all about us, there is a new kind of mentoring needed today. We who are immigrants in the postmodern world need young mentors, natives, who will help us learn the language, paradigms, challenges, and issues of this new day. Thus, as never before, mentoring should be a two-way street, with older and younger colleagues connecting with one another, developing these two-way mentoring relationships for the sake of the whole church.

7

The Crisis in Governance of "Mainline" Churches

The World War II generation shaped, or significantly reshaped, most forms of congregational and denominational governance currently in use in "mainline" communions. While technical adjustments to these forms have been made from time to time during the past forty years, the essence of these forms has not changed substantially since the post–WWII era of the 1940s through the 1960s. They continue to reflect the WWII generation's appetite for "being involved" in the decision-making processes of these institutions, a love for "direct" democracy.

Literally, "direct democracy" means everyone has a vote, in contrast to "indirect" or "representative democracy," in which the authority to make decisions is delegated to certain groups of representatives (boards, committees, house, senate, assembly, etc.).

While it is most often only the smallest of congregations that have true "direct democracy" in governance (all members vote on all questions), even the "representative" forms of governance found in most mainline institutions still reflect the WWII generational ethos of "being involved" by knowing what is happening and having a voice. Thus, "representational" boards, committees, and so forth still tend to be very large in size. It is not unusual for congregations of five hundred active members to have a board of seventy-five or more. These very large governing bodies are reticent to give very much authority to the smaller groups, which are sometimes formed to facilitate decision making. These smaller groups, then, are usually created to investigate matters and to bring recommendations to the larger group, but are seldom empowered to make significant decisions *on behalf* of the larger group.

Denominational examples also abound. When the Disciples are seeking a new general minister and president, a representative search committee of fifteen members is appointed to conduct a search process. However, this committee must bring two to five names to the larger "Administrative Committee" (forty-four members) rather than one name. Thus, the larger body reserves the primary decision making for itself. Some other mainline denominations bring multiple candidates to the entire synod or assembly, a practice they would never encourage in congregations.

These large governing bodies worked reasonably well until the mid-1960s, because there was until then a "social consensus" in the United States. That is, there was a "mainline ethos," which was a White Anglo-Saxon Protestant male ethos: *the Establishment*. Nearly everyone recognized it and deferred to it, even those who were not part of it (including women, people of color, and those of ethnicities other than Euro-American). People "knew their place" in this scheme of things, *the Understanding*, and acted accordingly or suffered powerful sanctions. People of color were lynched for violating *the Understanding*. Women and children were beaten under the tacit authority of *the Understanding*. During WWII, Japanese Americans were subject to internment for fear they might take advantage of the moment to seek the overthrow of *the Establishment*. This list goes on to our collective national shame.

In the words of the Declaration of Independence, "We hold these truths to be self-evident, that all *men* are created equal." While we rightly understand and appreciate that in the eighteenth century this statement was revolutionary in its inference, it also reflects the bigotries of the day. "Men" meant "white men." It did not include women or people of color. It was nearly a hundred years before the thirteenth amendment ended slavery (1865), and two more amendments were required to ensure the rights of former slaves (the fourteenth in 1868 and the fifteenth in 1870). Women did not receive the right to vote until 1920 (the Nineteenth Amendment). No Roman Catholic could be elected President until 1960, and we have not yet elected a Jew, a woman, a Hispanic, or a person of color to that high office. But it was not until the Civil Rights Act of 1964 and the Voter Rights Act of 1965 that the WASP "mainline" culture really began to come unglued. It was accelerated by dissent regarding the Vietnam War and by the development of mass media and, later, globalization.

Apart from its moral inadequacies, this "social consensus," "mainline ethos," or *Understanding* made decision making rather simple, as opinions that did not represent it didn't have to be taken seriously. But today, there is much more diversity at the tables of governance, and many more voices are being heard, albeit imperfectly. Even in mainline congregations and other mainline organizations that are overwhelmingly of a single racial or ethnic group, women are increasingly being heard, in many cases for the first time. In mainline denominations, people of color and ethnicity are also being heard in a way they were not before and with a new freedom to express their own inherited ethos rather than the "mainline ethos." These "new" participants in the conversation at once bring a much richer context out of which decisions can be made *and* the need for new ways of making those decisions to insure that everyone can be heard.

Modern versus Postmodern Church Governance

As a consultant, I frequently encounter congregations that have huge governing boards. These boards are products of the love affair of WWII-generation folks with participatory, direct democracy.[1] But such large boards seldom serve well today.

Often, such a board will have only about 30 percent in attendance, or about twenty to twenty-five individuals. In contrast to those members who created these bodies several decades ago, current members figure that, with so many people on the board, their personal presence doesn't matter much. They also know that such a large board isn't going to be making many important decisions but will, usually, be rubber-stamping decisions that have already been made by leadership or by a smaller group.

About the only time a large percentage of board members show up is on those relatively rare occasions when something that actually seems to be *interesting* comes up. This most often means *when there is a controversy.* This is unfortunate because, since attendance is usually so low, the group is not usually building the sense of community that could make it possible for them to work well together on resolving a difficult issue. In any case, it is extremely difficult for a mass meeting of seventy-five people or more to work through a conflict creatively. The tendency is for board members (and often a number of non-board members) to show up, "vent their spleens," and then participate in a divisive vote that will result in "winners and losers."

Such large boards worked better fifty years ago because most of the members showed up meeting after meeting. They *enjoyed* board meetings. This is something that strikes most Baby Boomers and nearly all Baby Buster and Millennial folks as rather bizarre. These post–WWII generations tend to see board meetings as, at best, a necessary evil, not as a privilege or as "fun." Today, the people of younger generations often volunteer to engage in direct service projects, but as for going to a board or committee meeting, sticking needles in their eyeballs would be higher on their list of things to do in their spare time.

Today, a smaller board of perhaps fifteen members, who understand themselves as *representing* the others in the congregation and representing the work of the board *to* the others in the congregation (rather than merely representing their own opinions) will better serve a church of five hundred or larger. Why?

First, because a well-led board of up to fifteen people or less will usually attract attendance that is 85 percent or higher. The members of such a board view their individual presence as important because each one represents a significant percentage of the whole and because smaller numbers mean that each member gets ample opportunity to speak to issues and doesn't have to fight to get the floor.

Second, the higher percentage of regular attendance means that a sense of community can develop among members. Participation in the group becomes *emotionally significant.* This makes for more positive and constructive meetings.

Third, a smaller board is usually able to make decisions by consensus rather than by debate and vote. Consensus does not mean "unanimity," but means that every member of the board can support a particular decision even if it is not his or her first choice. Such decisions, in turn, lead the whole congregation toward unity rather than division.

However, in order for such a smaller board to work best, the members must understand that their role is *representative* rather than *direct.*

In *direct* democracy, people go to a meeting to represent their own point of view. One thinks of the town hall meetings of old New England. Citizens went, expressed their opinion, and voted. Most accepted the decisions of the majority whether they personally agreed with the decision or not because they lived in the community and really had no alternative but to abide by the decision (unless they chose to move away to a different town). Most decisions were made with large margins of approval because there was a "social consensus" that most citizens accepted as an appropriate basis for decision making. However, today there is no generally accepted social consensus. People today bring widely diverging ideas and perspectives to almost every question. (One of the chief marks of the postmodern era is such a wide divergence of perspectives and personally held "truths.")

In *representative* democracy, each member of the board stands for the voices and opinions of a segment of the congregation. When a representative board is at its best: (1) the congregation is kept informed and aware of the kinds of issues that are being discussed; (2) the board members solicit opinions from, and listen carefully to, the members of the congregation and bring to the table every opinion they have heard across the life of the congregation; (3) through dialogue, the board seeks to gather all the wisdom they can from all the opinions they hear; and, finally, (4) in dialogue the board seeks to arrive at consensus or near-consensus decisions that reflect as much of the wisdom of the various points of view as is possible. These decisions are then reported in a timely fashion to the congregation with a thorough rationale. If there are minority points of view on the board, these are also reported.

It may be argued that developing such consensus or near-consensus takes a lot of time and energy. Perhaps, but it doesn't take as much time and energy as cleaning up after "win-lose" decisions that divide and alienate, failing to take into account the wisdom of minority points of view. By creating *congruence and common commitment* in congregational life, the process actually creates positive energy.

Again, such a board that is smaller in size needs to be very intentional about keeping the rest of the congregation informed about the issues being considered. The board may want to schedule one or more "hearings" (no decisions to be made at such a meeting) for the members of the congregation to express their opinions in the presence of the whole board to be certain they are heard accurately. Alternatively, or in addition, the board may ask the members of the congregation to participate in a survey or to participate in "listening groups." The more the congregation knows about the issues being addressed and the more they feel their points of view are being heard, the more trust there is and the more likely it is that a consensus decision will be accepted and honored by the whole congregation.

The *temptation* for a smaller board will be to short circuit the consensus-building process by "over-trusting" the judgment of certain key leaders (including the pastor) and thus failing to adequately listen to, or communicate with, the congregation. However, if the board fulfills its representative responsibilities, and adequately communicates with the whole congregation before and after decisions, the congregation will be able to move forward together and with greater energy than can be accomplished through an over-sized and under-functioning board.

What about Denominational Decision Making?

In denominational structures, the intensity of fellowship and community (and thus trust) is usually not nearly as powerful as in a congregation. This means, in part, that denominational leadership must be sure that all the various diversities of the denomination's membership (in terms of race, ethnicity, age, and breadth of opinion) are at every table where ideas and proposals are being developed. It is not enough to invite diversity to the table only after a proposal has been fully conceived and developed. The diversity of the denomination must be there from the beginning of the development of a proposal. In determining who should be at the table representing the diverse membership, the formal and/or informal leaders of each constituent group should be consulted.

Most mainline denominations have formulas to insure that people of all races and ethnicities are part of decision making. These old formulas typically call for denominational committees and governing bodies to be composed in such a way that at least 20 percent of the group comprises people of color and ethnicity other than Euro-American. However, if the mainline denominations understand the United States to be their primary mission field, then their committees and governing bodies will need to move toward reflecting the demographics of the continent they are seeking to reach—not only in terms of racial ethnic presence, but also in terms of generational presence. The demographic trend calls for a rethinking of the old formulas in a way that helps mainline denominations make the transition from being predominantly white and older to being truly reflective of North American demographics today.

The 20 percent figure itself presupposes that "racial ethnic minorities" are a monolithic category, when each demographic group is actually filled with diversity. African Americans and Haitian Americans, Philippine Americans and Chinese Americans, Guatemalan Americans and Cuban Americans are not simply interchangeable as "racial ethnic minority persons." There is great diversity among all the various racial ethnic groups and among the individuals themselves.

In this time of transition, such formulas help keep us *all* more honest in the face of the racism and generationalism that is so rampant in all mainline organizations. Yet, in the application of such formulas, there must also be a spirit of grace and deep appreciation for differences and not merely a kind of legalism.

It is also important, as noted above, that the breadth of opinion be represented at decision-making tables. The temptation is for denominational leadership to select *out* those who have an opinion different from their own so that the ultimate recommendation will represent their own opinion. This is a bad strategy. It is manipulative and will ultimately result in an undercutting of trust for denominational leaders and huge frustration on the part of those whose opinions were not represented in the formative stage of decision making. Such an approach assumes that the outcome of a vote is more important than the process of developing the decision.

More profound, perhaps, is the long held, but no longer true, underlying assumption that if a denominational body takes a prophetic stance (usually as defined by the leader or group who is manipulating the process), that stance will have an important impact on the society at large. This assumption is a holdover from the pre-1968 era. Society could care less about denominational pronouncements in and of themselves (except that society does have a prurient fascination with what such pronouncements represent in terms of the political fault lines present in a denomination). A more realistic assumption today is that a denomination has an impact on society primarily to the degree to which its members individually embrace, advocate, and live a particular point of view. Thus, the chief task of leadership becomes the education and transformation (rather than the manipulation) of the members themselves.

Are there times when denominational bodies must make pronouncements to the world that define what they regard as faithfulness and social justice? Of course, yes. But those pronouncements must not come as a product of political manipulation by church leadership. If they do, they will quickly be seen as such by both the citizenry and the nation's political leaders. As it is today, Washington politicians have access to sophisticated polling information so that they are well aware that the pronouncements of mainline church governance bodies seldom represent the majority (or even a significant minority) of the denomination's membership and thus may safely be dismissed as mostly irrelevant to the national political landscape.

This does not mean that a denominational leader should not personally address issues in a prophetic way. Indeed, I believe it is the *responsibility* of denominational leaders to speak prophetically both to the church and to the nation. However, it is one thing to speak in one's own voice and thus take responsibility for one's point of view. It is quite another thing to manipulate the church's governance so as to give the false impression that one is speaking for the body or so as to blunt the personal cost of one's own prophetic utterances.

What passes as "prophetic" ministry sometimes turns out to be an ineffective shortcut that avoids the hard work of effective Christian education. *Transformative* leadership seeks to bring members into a meaningful encounter with uncomfortable truth, not simply to bring simplistic resolutions to be voted for or against after a few minutes of mostly meaningless "public debate."

In the denominational setting, this will mean providing written materials that address the breadth of opinion regarding a particular subject; offering opportunities to hear from an array of informed speakers and having time for dialogue with the speakers and one another; and providing these kinds of resources and opportunities for boards, synods, assemblies, conventions, and, most importantly, congregations.

It will also mean changing governance procedures so that individual leaders, groups, or congregations cannot easily manipulate the denominational decision-making processes. Such changes will not only bring about a more authentic and effective social justice witness, but will also help protect the church from the politicizing strategies that often emanate from both ends of the ideological spectrum. In short, it will mean moving from a "democracy" paradigm to a "discernment" paradigm.

8

Seeing the Challenges through Polarities

In the face of the "perfect storm" that mainline denominations and their component organizations have been experiencing over the past forty years, I find it helpful to think about these issues in terms of "polarities." Few organizations are purely at "one or the other" end of a spectrum. Rather, most lie somewhere between the poles. Identifying where an organization is on a spectrum can be very instructive. Some of these polarities have already been mentioned.

Maintenance versus Mission

This is perhaps the most fundamental polarity of all: Where is an institution on the "maintenance versus mission" continuum? Organizations that lean toward the maintenance end of the continuum are most often driven by anxiety. Maintenance *becomes* the mission.

Organizations focused on maintenance tend to spend most of their time, energy, and other resources in self-preservation. For example, how many of the groups and activities of the institution are dedicated to governance, fund-raising, and up-keep of the building or other facilities versus outreach into the church, the community, and the world? How much activity is focused on those who are already members versus those who are not members or attendees? How many new congregations are being birthed and nurtured?

Organizations focused on maintenance tend to see even traditional aspects of the mission through the lens of maintenance. In working with congregations that are seeking fresh vision, I often ask them at a congregational gathering to tell me what their hopes are for the congregation. A typical response is something like, "More members...because if this

church is going to be here in fifty years, we have to have new members."
True enough, new members are necessary if a congregation is going to
be there for future generations. But such a maintenance-oriented church
will not attract younger people: they will be attracted by a congregation's
sincere desire to live and share the gospel and to meet the needs of people.
This represents real adaptive change.

Finance versus Stewardship

In congregations, a focus on maintenance is often exemplified and
nurtured by combining the functions of finance and stewardship into
the work of one committee. I am here using "finance" to mean the
development of proposed budgets, keeping an eye on income versus
expenses, and holding the organization accountable to fiscal responsibility. I am here using "stewardship" to mean educating the congregation
to give of their time, talent, and money; promoting tithing; giving
generously to the annual stewardship campaign; and encouraging people
to contribute from their accumulated resources to endowments and other
special funds—all as a matter of spiritual discipline. Ideally, the work of
"finance" is done as a function of stewardship.

However, when the finance and stewardship functions are put
together in one committee, I find that "finance" most often comes to be
regarded as a function separate from stewardship, and "finance" trumps
"stewardship" every time. That is, a "finance and stewardship committee" will always look for ways to "cut spending" before they will look
for ways to "increase giving." This is natural for a committee in a
congregation that is focused on maintenance because (1) it is hard for
most people to ask others for money and (2) when a committee is
primarily focused on money as a way of "keeping things going," it feels
disingenuous to ask members to contribute more money for mere
maintenance, especially when the members all have their own
maintenance needs at home. It is "natural" for a committee to seek ways
to encourage members to increase giving only when they are (1)
convinced that giving is a blessing to the givers and/or (2) that the
increased giving will help the institution be more *mission*-oriented rather
than merely maintenance-oriented.

Some have sought to address this by changing the name of the
committee from "Finance and Stewardship" to "Stewardship and
Finance." Yet that seldom does anything but perhaps create a momentary
illusion of change. Separating the two functions and putting them in the
hands of two different groups might be helpful, but only then if the
underlying issue is addressed: the congregation's focus on maintenance
rather than mission.

In middle judicatories and national agencies/structures, a focus on
maintenance can be detected when appeals for funds are made to

congregations and members based upon the needs of the judicatory/ agency *as an organization* rather than the needs of the *mission* that the judicatory/agency was created to address.

One can also see a focus on maintenance in judicatories/agencies that maintain oversized boards and committees. Such oversized bodies are always justified in terms of communication, but seldom is there any real plan for effectively communicating to congregations through the members of these governance bodies. The real (and usually unconscious agenda) is to keep the governance bodies so big that they are rendered incapable of actually being able to change anything and/or so they can be effectively controlled by primary leaders. Never underestimate the tendency of a system to use its own structures to maintain homeostasis nor its capacity to use even good leaders to do so.

Withholding Authority versus Granting Authority

In both congregations and denominational structures, another sign of anxiety and a focus on maintenance can be seen in the withholding of authority from leaders and committees to actually implement initiatives. Even a highly trusted individual leader will often find the authority to act is withheld because there is insufficient *trust* in the system to give authority to anybody. The tortured "reasoning" of the system, as it were, goes like this: "We don't trust anyone to change anything because if we trust them they will abuse that trust by actually *changing* something."

Another way to undercut authority, and thus to assure *maintenance*, is to provide unclear job descriptions for leaders, committees, or boards. A clear job description, in writing, properly approved by the appropriate governing body, grants a large measure of formal authority to do what the job description says. However, fuzzy job descriptions grant little authority because if no one really knows what someone is supposed to do, that person won't be able to do much of anything. He or she will be limited to *informal* authority, which is generally much more difficult and time- and energy-consuming to maintain and utilize than is *formal* authority.

In contrast, an organization that is focused on *mission* will typically have a clear understanding of what the mission of the organization is, will have right-sized governance bodies, will have clear job descriptions for leaders and governance bodies, and will hold leaders accountable to that mission and to their job descriptions.

Bill McKinney published a book in 1994 based on extensive interviews with denominational leaders of the 1970s and 1980s.[1] As the title of the book, *The Responsibility People,* implies, these denominational leaders felt a significant sense of responsibility for the faithfulness and health of their denominational systems. However, the interviews revealed that regardless of the polity within which these leaders served, they shared a sense of having very little real authority to carry out their responsibilities.

I believe this lack of authority was in some measure due to an underlying assumption of the modern era that the universe is a fixed, ultimately predictable reality that operates on the basis of certain immutable laws. If one can simply discover and understand these laws, then organizations can be created that will function effectively and need little more than an occasional "tweak." The church in the modern era created organizations that were assumed to be "right," and the implicit role of the leader in these modern institutions is simply to maintain the organization.

Likewise, most mainline congregations were organized or reorganized on the basis of modern assumptions. Again, the key assumption here is that all the organization of the congregation will ever need is an occasional tweak, and thus there is no reason to give anyone the authority necessary to change it more deeply. In my own experience as a "head of communion," even in the face of obvious dysfunctions, again and again I heard the same counsel from other leaders in the denominational system: "'The Design' (our Disciples' denominational "para-constitution") is not the problem. The problem is just people's failure to live out The Design as it was intended." An important moment of epiphany came to me one day late in my service as general minister and president. I finally realized that The Design, created in the mid 1960s, *no longer functions effectively*. That is, The Design no longer functions effectively unless you define "effective" as perpetuating the institution as it was in the modern era.

To be more accurate, the core values represented in the Preamble to The Design of the Disciples (and in the corresponding first pages of most of the foundational documents of most of the mainline denominations) are still generally valid and on target. These pages describe *who we are* as mainline churches, and these descriptions generally hold up from generation to generation. But the pages that follow, which describe the structures provided for the day-to-day work of the church are *time and culture bound* and do not have the same force as does the part of the foundational documents that deals with core values.

If 95 percent of a leader's energy is spent maintaining the system itself, I believe it is safe to say that the system is "broken" or at least ill-suited for the present context. I have had enough conversations with mainline "heads of communion" and middle judicatory leaders (as well as congregational ministers) to know that this is where most of the mainline churches live day to day. This is not simply because the finances are waning, though that certainly aggravates everything. It is because the fundamental organizations themselves are ill-suited for the postmodern era.

When I look at so many mainline church organizations, I am reminded of the grease factory that had no shipping department. It had no shipping department because it used all the grease it produced to grease the grease-making machines. Any organization that "has no shipping department" is due for a reconsideration of its purpose, approach, leadership, and governance.

Management versus Vision

In the modern era, organizational consultants identified three fundamental types of leaders: the visionary, the planner, and the bureaucrat (or manager). The idea was that a "visionary" would establish an innovative purpose for the organization, then a "planner" would adapt the organization to serve that visionary purpose, and finally a succession of bureaucrats (managers) would keep the machine oiled and running smoothly. Recognizing the Second Law of Thermodynamics (things run down because of friction and such), it was further theorized that after a number of years of operation, the organization would need to repeat the cycle of visionary, planner, and manager in order to continue running smoothly and productively.

A corresponding modern assumption, then, was that a single vision might empower an organization for more than a generation. However, in the postmodern world, the social context changes so rapidly that visions typically have a useful life of closer to something like five to ten years at maximum. This means, in part, that leaders seldom have the luxury of being merely one or another of the three kinds of leader. Today, leaders must be able to function effectively as all three: visionary, planner, and manager.

Obsolete organizations, in their anxiety, often desire that their leaders be managers when vision and planning is needed. In the church, this is expressed in the longing of dying congregations for "a young minister who will come and help us grow again by doing the things ministers used to do." What they really need is a leader who can embody all three approaches.

However, it must be added that the church typically does not develop leaders proficient in all three approaches. Thus, leaders tend to operate only out of their *natural* propensity rather than having the flexibility to operate out of each of the three approaches as appropriate and needed.

As a consequence, we have visionaries who do not know how to help a congregation or denominational organization move past envisioning to the corresponding organizational development and operation. Likewise, and perhaps more frequently, we have managers who do not know how to help a congregation or denominational organization do appropriate visioning and planning.

The default position is most often "manager," because that is what the anxious organization wants: someone to "manage" things till the storm passes. Of course, the storm hasn't passed and, given the incredibly rapid social change that is such a feature of the postmodern era, it looks like it is going to be stormy for a long time to come.

Thus, in these modern systems that are trying to "hold on" during this postmodern time, the tendency for one-dimensional leaders is this: the "visionary" most often "crashes and burns" or "burns out"; the "planner" fails because a plan made for an obsolete organization is just so much "rearranging of deck chairs on the Titanic"; the "manager" burns out from a sense of boredom and futility. This describes too many clergy (and laity) today.

Organizations will not move from "management to mission" without effective leadership. The move requires vision (having vision is different from "having a vision statement"). The move also requires primary leaders that have the capacity to operate out of all three leadership approaches (visionary, planner, manager). Since few individual leaders are able to operate out of all three, this usually means a team of people with complementary leadership styles working together, some or most of whom may be recruited volunteers.

Pragmatism versus Core Values

"Pragmatism" is an approach that measures ideas and concepts on the basis of their practical results. At its best, it is the "can do" in which Americans pride themselves. At its worst, it assumes that the "ends justify the means." The primary question becomes not, "Is it right?" but, "Will it work?" But because it *is* a moral universe, most often *the end is shaped by the means*, whether we wish this were true or not.

Nature has a way of maintaining its own integrity. In biology it is called deoxyribonucleic acid: DNA. If you plant corn, you reap corn. If you plant beans, you get beans. However, pragmatism has a way of substituting results that insure *survival* for results that have *integrity*. Pragmatism encourages technical fixes rather than any adaptive change that is needed. In the short run, this may produce stunning results…like fertilizer piled around a plant that is growing in bad soil. But sooner or later, the wise farmer knows that the poor soil itself must be addressed if the farm is to have a future.

A key responsibility of leadership is to help an institution constantly clarify, reaffirm, and live out its core values, which are its "DNA." There are the core values that the institution was created to serve. But there may also be some unconscious, or at least unarticulated, core values that actually function in place of, or over against, the "official" or original core values.

For example, an inherited core value of all the mainline denominations is the gospel of Jesus Christ. However, an unconscious core value may be "respectability": that is, making members feel respectable. This is a grave danger in denominations that in some ways have become more closely identified with the culture than with the gospel. Even a casual reading of history demonstrates that faithful Christianity is often, maybe usually, at odds with its host culture.[2] As institutions decline, they frequently begin to prize survival above all else. Of course, survival *is* a key to continued service. But survival is not the most important thing for institutions dedicated to the service of Christ. Indeed, Christ is constantly calling us to a cross: "Those who want to save their life will lose it, and those who lose their life for my sake will find it" (Mt. 16:25). This is not a call to suicide, either for individuals or institutions, but it *is* a call to integrity, a call to remain true to the values of the gospel even when it threatens to end life or, at least, life as we have known it personally or institutionally.

A congregation that begins as a "mission station" in an urban neighborhood may gradually morph into an institution that prides itself on its beautiful steeple and stained-glass windows, and may thus become dedicated to the preservation of the building at all costs: including the loss of its own originating core values. A denominational bureau that was begun for the purpose of supporting congregations may gradually develop a sense of entitlement, a sense that congregations were created to support the *agency* in the manner to which it has become accustomed. The antidote for this loss of integrity, this loss of core values, is to keep the stated core values before the body, to regularly review the originating core values, and to regularly decide anew whether those values are still relevant or whether new core values should be embraced.

In addition to staying clear about the core values, the leadership must help the institution develop ways and means that reflect those values. This means avoiding pragmatic short cuts that may speed results but that ultimately undercut the integrity of the results.

Membership versus Discipleship

When a church is focused on maintenance rather than mission, it focuses on the number of members it has rather than on the number of disciples it is shaping and nurturing. Telltale signs of this include attitudes toward denominational yearbook numbers. All the mainline denominations request congregations to report for their yearbooks the number of people baptized/confirmed and the number of people received into membership by transfer from another congregation or denomination. Congregations focused on maintenance tend to be concerned only with the net total number of members compared with last year and, especially, how many members joined by transfer of membership this year. Though baptisms and confirmations are seen as good, they are also generally assumed to involve children and youth, and children and youth are unable to contribute much financially to the institutional strength of the church. Though there are significant numbers of American adults who have never been baptized, few *maintenance-* oriented congregations think of adults as primary subjects of the congregation's evangelistic mission because they see their mission to be maintenance rather than bringing people, even adult people, to discipleship.

Likewise, maintenance-oriented congregations tend to focus on assimilating people into *membership* rather than focusing upon assimilating people into *faith* and *into the body of Christ*. Part of this is that most mainline congregations are still operating on the assumption (left over from pre-1968 days) that the culture at large still transmits the language and concepts of mainline Christian faith. Thus, it is assumed that "everyone knows the content of the faith, they just aren't all members of the church." This is why mainline churches, of all the various expressions of the church of Jesus Christ, typically spend the *least* amount of time with educational activities such as Sunday school or other *equipping* classes and events. This is also a key to understanding why so many mainline Christians have such difficulty knowing what they believe and think as Christians about various matters (or why they are so easily swayed by secular arguments from the culture in general, politicians and radio talk show hosts in particular). It is also why so many mainline Christians have such a hard time *sharing* their faith, and the inability to share the faith creates a vicious circle that further weakens the church.

If ever there was a time for *teaching and discipling,* this is it. But churches focused on maintenance seldom spend much energy on teaching and discipling because it does require energy and does not *immediately* impact the maintenance of the organization (though the absence of teaching and discipling *will* impact the maintenance of the organization before long).

Dependency versus Capacity

Those institutions that are focused on survival and maintenance have a vested interest in keeping people dependent upon them, so that they will be *necessary* and will *survive*. This is one reason why so many ministers engage in a pastor-centered style: it alleviates their anxiety about not being needed. This is why when so many middle judicatories and national church bureaus "serve" congregations, they do it in a way that seeks to make judicatories and bureaus seem necessary and irreplaceable, that is, in a way that seeks to make congregations dependent upon them.

Leaders of congregations, middle judicatories, and national church bureaus that are focused on *mission* seek to do their work in a way that builds *capacity* in their members and congregations. Capacity means members are nurtured by the congregation into being able to read the Bible and think for themselves about what it may mean and how it may be applied to life. It means members develop a prayer life that empowers them to interact directly with God and not just through the pastor. It means members are encouraged to find a ministry to which they feel called and that the congregation supports these lay-ministers.

Capacity means the middle judicatory and national church bureaus nurture a congregation into connection with other congregations and with wider networks of resources. Thus a congregation can become a learning organization and not always be dependent on the middle judicatory or the national structure for programs and leadership.

Control versus Empowerment

Akin to "capacity versus dependency," *control versus empowerment* means that a leader nurtures the faith and spiritual gifts of members in such a way that they can think for themselves and can themselves become teachers and leaders.

One may reasonably ask, "Why do clergy not provide training and support for their lay spiritual leaders?" There are many answers. Some clergy are themselves fully captive to secular approaches and thus do not themselves understand the need for lay spiritual leadership. Some clergy feel that disempowering lay spiritual leaders, or keeping them dependent, will enhance their own ability as clergy to lead and control (which begs the question, "Exactly whose kingdom are we trying to build?"). Some clergy just don't know how to train and support.

We live in an age of specialization. As a friend of mine used to joke, "We live in an era when more and more people know more and more about less and less, so that most of us know practically everything about almost nothing!" One consequence of specialization is that many laypeople come to church already feeling incompetent in matters of the Spirit and of church life. It is only as their capacity to function as deeply Christian people is enhanced, and their partnership with clergy is nurtured, that the church itself can reach its potential.

Democracy versus Discernment

The mainline churches, by definition, grew up within a framework of American democracy. And, as we have seen, there was a further democratization of the mainline churches in the 1940s and 1950s. In its love for democracy, the modern mainline church has forgotten the difference between *democracy* and *discernment*. To offer simple definitions, one could say that "democracy" seeks to know the will of the members, while "discernment" seeks to know the will of God. But having lost much of their spiritual depth to cultural captivity, mainline churches tend to treat the will of the members (expressed in votes) as being the *same* as the will of God.

Thus the unspoken axiom of the mainline has become, "What is the will of God in regard to this or that matter? We don't know, so let's vote on it and see." This axiom is the assumption in every "modern" business meeting of the church: board meetings, congregational meetings, middle judicatory and denominational gatherings.

There is, of course, a place for both democracy and discernment. Some questions do not require discernment: God probably doesn't care much what color the fellowship hall is to be painted, so a simple democratic polling of the committee will do.

On the other hand, discernment most often needs to be affirmed by some kind of democratic decision. For example, if a person believes she has discerned a call to ministry, she cannot simply declare herself "ordained." In all the mainline traditions, her discernment must be reviewed and voted on by her local congregation and must be affirmed by the wider denomination through a vote of a commission on ministry or some such representative group.

Discernment is not simple or easy, and no one can ultimately claim to know the mind of God infallibly in regard to any matter. Thus, a democratic process of review and decision is provided to assure that at least the majority of those who have the responsibility to decide concur that true discernment has occurred (though such decisions must be made with the utmost of humility). No doubt, sometimes the church makes the wrong decision in this regard, but it is the best way we know to insure the integrity of the processes of discernment.

As with a person's discernment of a call to ministry, the collective discernment of church leaders about a matter of importance to the body usually has to be confirmed by a representative group or, in some cases, by the whole body via a democratic process of review and decision. But often, issues that would most appropriately be treated as matters of discernment are instead taken to the governing bodies for debate and vote without the benefit of any discernment process. Thus, mainline churches approach some of the most significant issues of the day by seeking to know the will of the members without substantially considering what might be the mind of God. So, for example, discussions about homosexuality have tended to become a matter of argument on the basis of personal feelings. Our feelings are often rooted in our own deep insecurities and there is no greater point of vulnerability, fear, and pain for most people than human sexuality. Though the Bible is often quoted in such arguments, it is much more often quoted as a "proof text" than in a way that invites or reflects a deep struggle with the context and meaning of the text itself.

Most every mainline congregation has laypeople appointed to do the work of discernment, in partnership with the clergy. However, as mainline congregations have become increasingly "secularized," these lay spiritual leaders have become increasingly dysfunctional or consumed by involvement in democracy *instead* of discernment. It is easy to see how this happens. First, it follows the larger cultural drift toward secular approaches. Second, in the absence of training and support (the nurturing of lay capacity) from clergy, these lay leaders naturally drift into doing work they feel more qualified to do and more comfortable doing (which is almost anything other than spiritual leadership.) Thus, those laypersons appointed to be the spiritual leaders of a congregation tend to shy away from discernment in favor of more mundane tasks, and thus the body loses much of its spiritual power.

In my own communion, we have lay "elders" elected by each congregation to serve in this role (they have other spiritual and pastoral responsibilities as well, including presiding at the communion table). However, through the last half of the twentieth century, the traditional work of elders as "spiritual leaders" faded away in most congregations and the elders have become mostly ceremonial leaders at the communion table. I find a key to the renewal of Disciples congregations is the recreation of a significant role for these displaced elders, which addresses the current context (and does not assume that the nineteenth century role should simply be recovered or replicated).

A church that has no training in or practice of the spiritual disciplines will find discernment very difficult. It requires prayerful study and reflection, it requires humility, and it requires relationship with God and openness to the Holy Spirit. These are things we all want, but which are actually antithetical to the culture in which we live and to the culture of most of our institutions.

In 1995, I introduced the idea of using "processes of discernment" instead of General Assembly resolutions in regard to particularly complex and controversial issues. It garnered strong emotional reactions: some defending the "debate and vote" methodology of assembly resolutions and some expressing hunger for a new way to do public witness. Almost everyone demonstrated that they take the denomination's public witness seriously.

My concern was that our denominational pronouncements (by national assemblies, synods, and conventions) are so often products of mere democracy. These bodies have dispatched some of the most important issues of the day with a few minutes of debate and a quick vote. Does anyone really learn anything in these processes? Do our either-or, up-or-down votes really result in the best and most thoughtful statements? I believe they often do not.

A summary of my personal hope for our public witness as mainline denominations in this time of "disestablishment" is that we could: (1) help congregations as well as individuals engage in more effective witness; (2) provide individuals, congregations, and whole denominations opportunities for serious study and dialogue regarding the "weightier matters of the law: justice and mercy and faith" (Mt. 23:23); (3) foster *reflection and action* rather than merely issuing statements; and (4) make more effective use of our churches' educational resources (including college and seminary faculties).

Resolutions, as they are handled in most of our national gatherings, are seldom effective methods of education. But if they involved real discernment, they *could be* part of an effective method of helping our culturally captive membership struggle with the implications of the gospel in fresh ways and help them bring their lives more fully into congruence with those implications. Taken seriously, such an approach represents a radically new way of being and doing church, a way that is better suited to these postmodern times than the ways we have inherited from the 1950s and 1960s.

Additional resources regarding how to develop and implement processes of discernment include: *Holy Conversations: Strategic Planning as a Spiritual Practice for Congregations*, by Gil Rendle and Alice Mann (Alban Institute, 2003) and *Discerning God's Will Together: A Spiritual Practice for the Church*, by Danny Morris and Charles Olsen (Upper Room Books, 1997).

PART III

Leading a Journey of Transformation

How does one actually lead adaptive change in mainline churches? Remember that what we are seeking is not merely a destination. Rather, as leaders of adaptive change, we are seeking to lead our institutions into an ongoing journey of transformation. It is ongoing because our context is constantly changing, and thus our goals are constantly moving out ahead of us like a "pillar of cloud by day...and...a pillar of fire by night" (Ex. 13:21). A journey of transformation is, for both the leader and the institution, a way of *being* as much as it is a way of *doing*.

Therefore, we will begin by looking at some personal aspects of adaptive leadership and then move toward the "how to" of leading adaptive change.

9

Personal Aspects of Leading Adaptive Change

We have sought to analyze some of the challenges confronting mainline churches and why these institutions are as they are. However, as we begin thinking about how to lead adaptive change, let us begin by thinking about our own preparation and ourselves.

The demands placed on organizational leaders of all kinds these days are great. But the demands on leaders of declining institutions are enormous. When one assumes a role of leadership in a mainline denomination these days (whether in middle judicatory or national offices), it is like jumping into a huge ocean whirlpool: you must start swimming and you must swim fast. The initial rush of energy that comes to most of us from the sense of honor and affirmation at having been chosen for such a role may power a person for a few months. But it is not long before one is drawn into a struggle for personal as well as institutional survival. The more anxious and unhealthy the system, the more one is constantly being pushed, pulled, bypassed, and manipulated. Nowhere is the adage more true: "When you are up to your hips in alligators, it is hard to remember that the original objective was to drain the swamp!"

Most people who are chosen for these roles, and who feel *called* to these roles, are pastors: persons with deep sensitivities to the feelings of those around them. In every mainline organization with which I am familiar, the atmosphere is so emotionally charged as to be overwhelming to the pastoral heart. Yet, as pastors, their natural tendency is to want to engage the feelings of those around them at a *heart* level. Thus there is the challenge of remaining emotionally connected while maintaining one's legitimate and necessary emotional boundaries. One can speak of this as engaging the pastoral *head* so as not to deplete the pastoral *heart*.

Yet, as the inevitable weariness of long hours and too much travel sets in, it is harder and harder to maintain the necessary personal differentiation.

This means it is absolutely essential that the leader engage in the spiritual and personal disciplines. This certainly includes the spiritual disciplines of Bible study, prayer, silence, and regular worship in a place where one is not the leader. It also means a discipline of time with family, time with friends, and establishing an effective peer group.

Many mainline ministers in whatever setting (including congregations) have never established such spiritual and personal disciplines for themselves. This is a prescription for vocational, professional, and moral failure. In denominational leadership, where one does not even have the benefit of experiencing the rhythm of the church year, it can be deadly to the spirit.

As I look around the landscape of leadership in the mainline these days, I see four kinds of ministers.

The first group, perhaps one-third of all mainline ministers, is bright, well educated and well motivated, but constantly running on the edge of exhaustion and burnout. Many who are reading this book will recognize themselves as members of this group, desperately seeking a new model for ministry, a model that is effective and sustainable.

The second group, perhaps one-fourth of mainline ministers, is well educated and *was* well motivated, but has crossed over the line into burnout and clinical depression. They are going through the motions, but their passion for ministry has died and they go on in ministry primarily because they don't know what else to do. They probably will not see themselves here because, for the most part, they have stopped reading and, for the most part, trying.

The third group is relatively small: perhaps only 10 percent of mainline ministers. These are the ones who, by any reasonable measure, are incompetent. However, they *are* happy!

The fourth group, perhaps one-fourth of mainline ministers (but growing), is bright, well educated, well motivated, and have begun to figure out how to do ministry in a way that is life-giving and energizing, even though ministry is *always* hard work.

The question we are interested in is this: "How can more of us move into this fourth category and how can we give effective leadership to the mainline churches as they move from "captivity to modernity" into a faithful and effective life in these postmodern times?"

Perhaps the first word in leading adaptive change anywhere is *humility*.

Most of us are products of the very cultures we seek to change. Most of us grew up in a mainline church, and so we were encouraged, called, and educated through a mainline denomination. By the time most of us come to leadership in a mainline institution, the culture of the very generation that raised us up and believed in us has become part of the problem.

This means that much of what we are struggling to change in our institutions is also very much a part of ourselves. We are something like adolescent children struggling to differentiate from their parents. Children are at once so much *like* their parents, and yet know that they have to find their own way into a future that will be and must be different from their parents'. It is at times a hard, frustrating journey, but one that is made easier if as adolescents we do not allow ourselves to turn our frustration with ourselves and our parents into arrogance and anger. The more angry, arrogant, and rebellious adolescents become, the more difficult it is for parents to loosen their grip and to allow their children to shape their own lives. The more angry, arrogant, and rebellious we become as we seek to lead adaptive change in mainline churches, the more resistant the institution will become and the more we will become alienated from ourselves as well. Indulging our own infantile anger, arrogance, and rebellion sets us up for a fall.

The Challenge Confronting Late Moderns

Most of us in ministry today grew up in, or were shaped by, the late modern era (the late 1950s into the 1970s). This means that most of us in significant ways think like modern people. As some have said, while our children are *natives* of the postmodern era, we who were born in the modern era are *immigrants* in the postmodern era. This does not disqualify us from being effective leaders, nor does it make us irrelevant. It does, however, present some challenges with which we must struggle.

One of these challenges is our inherited mechanistic view of the world. We break things down to their various parts and look for the problems there. A native postmodern person tends to see the system as a whole and tends to address the whole rather than the parts.

There were those even in the eighteenth century who had already begun to critique the modern era's tendency toward reductionism, seeing everything as a collection of parts rather than as a dynamic whole. I love a little poem by William Wordsworth, "The Tables Turned: An Evening Scene, on the Same Subject," in which he makes the case for seeing the dynamic whole of a thing rather than the mere sum of its parts." One particularly pithy line in the poem reads,

"Our meddling intellect
Misshapes the beauteous forms of things;
We murder to dissect."[1]

We who are late-moderns were raised to dissect everything. It is a powerful approach to observation and discovery. It got us to the moon and back. However, it must be admitted in the end that most things are more than the sum of their parts.

In high school biology class, most of us "murdered to dissect" frogs, putting them in a closed jar with chloroform. We thought that by dissecting these creatures, we were learning about frogs. But the truth is, we were learning about dead frogs, which are much less than the hopping, swimming, croaking reality we experience as live frogs.

We tend to apply the same method to social systems, including church systems. We dissect them, pulling part from part, seeking to find "what makes it go as it does." This approach is not without value, but the corrective is to recognize that a system is more than the sum of its parts, that it is what it is and does what it does because of the interplay of the parts within a unique whole that cannot ultimately be divided or dissected.

The modern approach, reducing a system to its various parts, will nearly always encourage technical change and will nearly always miss the need for adaptive change. Adaptive change comes as we are willing to see the whole, to understand the essence of the thing as more than the sum of its parts.

A strictly modern analysis alone will not reveal much of what we need to know about a church system. The "consultant" role is a modern one, in which someone from "outside" the organization comes in to analyze the system in its various parts and pieces and to make recommendations as to how to "fix" this or that. This stereotypical "consultant" is so prevalent that I have sought to find a word other than *consultant* to describe what I understand my role to be as one who "comes alongside" church systems to help them to greater health and wholeness. I call myself a "coach-consultant" as a way of trying to differentiate from the old mechanistic, modern consultant approach. But I have yet to find the single word that adequately communicates an approach that is appropriate in this era.

Both approaches have value: an approach that examines the parts and an approach that sees the whole. The challenge for us late moderns is that we are schooled by our generation's culture in seeing the parts almost to the exclusion of seeing the whole. Thus, we tend to see everything in terms of "fix" rather than "health and wholeness." As someone said, "When all you have is a hammer, everything looks like a nail!"

What this all means in my own experience is that I constantly have to remind myself to look not only at the parts (though this has some value), but to look at the whole as well. I have to remind myself that I am not a mechanic fixing an engine by changing out parts, I am a physician seeking to help the healing of an organism—because church systems are more like organisms than they are like engines.

Again, it is not that technical change (fixing a problem within a system) is bad and adaptive change (addressing the system itself) is good. Each has its place. Analysis of the parts and analysis of the whole are both useful. The effective leader of adaptive change in the mainline church must understand each kind of change and know when each is appropriate. There is nearly always a mix of technical and adaptive change that is needed. The challenge to us late-moderns is to avoid doing technical change *thinking it is actually adaptive change.*

Whether we are immigrants in this postmodern era or natives, *humility* is the first word.

Humility is the beginning of all true spirituality. This is why Micah said (6:8), "what does the LORD require of you / but to do justice, and to love kindness, and to *walk humbly with your God?* (author's emphasis). This is why, in the Sermon on the Mount, Jesus placed the first beatitude where he did, first: "Blessed are the poor in spirit." (Mt. 5:3), or, more helpfully translated from the Greek, "Blessed are those who recognize their spiritual poverty" or "their spiritual need."

We rightly come to God as "disciples" (students), not as consultants. Humility, then, means approaching church systems as students and learners, rather than assuming we come with all the answers. Having all the answers is, after all, a modern quest. We come, then, seeking wisdom rather than absolute truth.

There are four personal aspects of leading adaptive change in mainline churches that we need to consider carefully: the theological, the spiritual, the physical, and the emotional.

The Theological Aspect

Most simply, theology means thinking about God in a logical way. Every effective mainline minister needs a theology that is powerful enough to help people make some sense out of the world as it is today. I believe in theological education, and I believe it should continue throughout our lives.

Some people go to seminary primarily in order to get a degree so they can be ordained. These folks have a remarkable capacity to attend 84–90 hours of graduate level classes without ever being touched by the experience. They don't *get* seminary. They are like people who get As and Bs throughout three years of high school Spanish yet they graduate without being able to speak the language.

What's the point of *going* to seminary if one is not going to be engaged by it theologically? One might as well follow another route to ordination and save the considerable time and money involved in a seminary education.

When I entered seminary, I went because that's what you had to do to get the credentials necessary for ordination. I hardly remember what I was taking the first year because I was hard at work in the little church where I was the pastor. I figured my ministry took precedence over being a student.

At the beginning of my second year, however, I took a course entitled "Contemporary Preaching." It was an eye opener for me. Within two weeks I realized I couldn't preach a contemporary sermon because I didn't have an understanding of God that had anything to say to the issues of the day.

I dropped the preaching course, took introduction to theology, and began earnestly exploring the nature and character of God. It changed my life. I began to realize that as a seminarian, *being a student* was my primary ministry. What a privilege seminary is, a privilege unknown to most Christians. Not only did seminary introduce me to contemporary ways of thinking about God, but it also gave me the tools to continue in a life-long quest. Thanks be to God (and thanks be to the mainline churches that provided such an educational opportunity).

But our theological preparation only *begins* with seminary. We must continue to prepare ourselves theologically all our lives if we are to have a relevant word to speak to the church in each succeeding generation.

Though most of those in our audiences do not have the benefit of a seminary education, they are not stupid. As people of faith, or people seeking faith, they usually recognize a powerful contemporary word when they hear it. And while they may not be able to name exactly what's missing, most of them know when a powerful contemporary word is not being heard. Sermons comprised of mere sociological or psychological pabulum do not satisfy. They want theological meat on their spiritual bones.

No one can "hit a theological home run" every week, or with every at-bat. But deep speaks to deep, and no minister can claim to be faithful without going deep, year after year.

The Spiritual Aspect

As important as theology is, the Christian life is more than thinking about God. It is also being in relationship with God. It is connecting one's own spirit to the Spirit of God. Theology without spirituality is like a shell that washes up on the beach...it may be beautiful in its structure, but it is lifeless.

There has been a powerful movement in recent years to recover the language and practice of the spiritual disciplines. The mainline churches, in our mechanistic modernism, had strayed so far from these traditional disciplines that we had to go to other parts of Christ's church to recover them. The Roman Catholic tradition has been particularly helpful in this rediscovery.

My favorite definition of the spiritual disciplines is this: *practices whereby we open ourselves to being shaped by God.* These disciplines include prayer, Bible study, worship, stewardship, service, and hospitality to strangers. In the hectic, fast-paced lifestyle most of us live in this postmodern era, prayer and study are exceedingly difficult to do with disciplined regularity. The demands of anxious individuals and mainline institutions only add to the difficulty. Yet, there is no substitute for these disciplines.

We don't much like discipline. The world today reinforces our infantile desire to get "something for nothing," to follow the path of least resistance, to read no book, to delay no gratification, to follow no discipline. Nevertheless, the words of Jesus are still true: "Enter through the narrow gate; for the gate is wide and the road is easy that leads to destruction, and there are many who take it. For the gate is narrow and the road is hard that leads to life, and there are few who find it" (Mt. 7:13–14). Jesus is not here commending narrow-minded interpretations of the Scriptures. He is speaking of living a spiritually disciplined life. Many mainline ministers have not made a deposit in their spiritual bank account since seminary, and so have been writing "bad checks" for a long time.

In the face of the confusion and powerlessness we often feel in contemporary life, no wonder there have arisen so many "spiritualities" that claim that we are somehow connected to God but which never really *submit* to the Holy Spirit, never really touch the ground, never really address the world as we know it. These spiritualities want to skip Good Friday and move directly to Easter.

Empty vessels masquerading as spiritual leaders do not fool most laypeople. They know spiritual hollowness when they see it. Many have left the mainline churches for other traditions just so they can find the life of the Spirit for which they pine.

An essential part of leading adaptive change in mainline churches is a personal, authentic, and disciplined spirituality. It is essential to the maintenance of one's own health and perspective, and it is essential to empowering the mainline church to engage in the deep adaptive change it must make.

The Physical Aspect

Perhaps I just didn't listen or didn't "get it" when my high school coaches were trying to teach me that physical fitness is a key to one's mental, emotional, and spiritual capacity as an adult. I honestly don't remember any one of them teaching me these things. My memory is that everything focused on the sport of the season.

My coaches appeared interested only in getting me in shape to be an effective offensive tackle in the fall, basketball forward in the winter, and discus thrower in the spring. I don't remember anyone explaining how important fitness, rest, and nutrition were beyond the next game. As I remember it, the focus appeared to be on winning games, not helping me to develop as a physically fit individual.[2] However, I readily admit that I may have not been paying attention or putting two and two together.

Fortunately, this approach has totally changed in public schools today. But I can tell you that now that I am in my fifties, even *I* "get it." When I am regularly exercising and paying attention to rest and nutrition, when I am paying attention to the various messages my body sends me everyday, it makes a huge difference in the quality of my life and work. I think better, pray better, preach and teach better, have greater endurance, and experience deeper satisfaction when I am physically fit. I have come to see physical fitness as a spiritual discipline.

I have also come to see ministry as an athletic vocation. Paul drew on this image in 1 Corinthians 9:24–27.

There is no more emotionally and spiritually difficult work than leading adaptive change in mainline churches. The tensions and stresses associated with transformation work are immense and constant. Most of us "somatize" our stress in one way or another. That is, we express our nervous tensions *in our bodies* in various ways. Some of us somatize our stress by sending it to our lower back, which results in lower back pain. Some of us send it to our shoulders and neck, to our digestive track, or to our cardio-vascular system.

Most of us have read the literature on "fight or flight." We were built in such a way that when we are confronted by a tiger or a bear, super-charging chemicals are produced by our glands and dumped into our bloodstream to enable us to have a burst of energy that will enable us either to fight successfully or to flee.

Well, few of us are confronted by actual tigers or bears these days (unless perhaps we are hiking on vacation), but these mainline churches are full of figurative tigers and bears, and most of us bring a whole psychic pantheon of tigers and bears with us from childhood into adulthood. Our brains have a hard time differentiating between fear and anxiety that is generated by actual wild animals and that generated by figurative or psychological wild animals. (Many of us don't just hit the ground running everyday...We hit the ground *being chased*.) It is all stress and it all calls forth an outpouring of blood-chemistry and temporary physical super-charging that has to go somewhere. Either we absorb it (which a physically fit body has some capacity to do), or we work it off physically, or, like a 110 volt light bulb screwed into a 220 volt circuit, we will be over-stressed and damage will ensue.

We tend to dismiss psychosomatic illness (illness that has its origins in the brain but which is "somatized," expressed in the body) saying, "It's all in your head." We do well to understand and appreciate that psychosomatic illness can kill us and, usually long before it kills us, renders us physically, mentally, emotionally, and spiritually ill and ineffective. This can be observed as a chronic condition in many of those "burned-out and clinically depressed" ministers of the second group.

In order to effectively lead adaptive change in mainline denominations, we need to be physically fit. I'm not talking about running marathons or bench-pressing 500 pounds. I am talking about the kind of physical fitness that keeps our body chemistry balanced and our cardio-vascular and skeletal-muscular systems healthy. Maintaining a healthy level of physical fitness is a quintessential part of "present[ing] [our] bodies as a living sacrifice,...which is [our] spiritual worship" (Rom. 12:1).

The Emotional Aspect

I don't know of anyone in *any* walk of life that does not have to deal with emotional issues. We all bring some of these with us from childhood. It is unavoidable, because being a part of the human condition means that we were raised by imperfect parents (just as we will ourselves be imperfect parents if we have children). And, in adulthood, we tend to find multiple ways in which to express these emotional issues.

We are all emotionally unbalanced to some degree. Part of the work of adulthood is to find greater balance, to learn what is real and what is not, to learn what is healthy and what is not. Seeking emotional wholeness is a life-long project and no one ever achieves complete emotional health.

This means we must all care for ourselves emotionally. Doing so is, I believe, another spiritual discipline. The struggle for emotional health unites us with all humanity and leads us to help others as they struggle with their own emotional demons. To neglect our emotional health is to invite burnout and inappropriate acting out of inner conflicts, anxieties, and past wounds.

For some of us, tending to our emotional health means finding and utilizing an effective mental health professional. As a pastor of congregations, I did a lot of pastoral counseling and referred scores of individuals to counselors in whom I had trust. But I consider it just as important a mark of caring professionalism that I have sought counseling myself at numerous points in my life.

We can struggle with our childhood issues alone, the hard way. Or, we can find and work with a qualified counselor, which is the easier way. We can struggle alone with the emotional stresses and strains that are so ubiquitous among those seeking to lead adaptive change in *any* organization, or we can surround ourselves with the emotional support of friends and family and, as needed, work with a qualified counselor. I have found that regular retreats, sometimes alone, most often with friends, have been life-changing and, sometimes, life-saving.

We are responsible for our own emotional health. This does not mean that we can or should "go it alone," or "just tough it out." It means we are responsible for finding and utilizing our own emotional resources. Though friends and family will sometimes suggest that we need help and try to lead us to water, no one but we ourselves can decide to drink of the healing waters fully and deeply.

As I read back over these last few pages, I realize that it sounds a bit "preachy." It reminds me of something I learned a long time ago:

preachers preach with the greatest energy when they are speaking to their own weaknesses. Over the years I have struggled with each of these four personal issues. I have struggled to keep fresh and current in my reading and thinking about the nature of God; I have struggled to practice the spiritual disciplines with consistency and devotion; I have struggled to stay on a program of regular exercise, being faithful for a few months and then neglecting my exercise for several weeks or months before picking it up again; and I have sometimes tried to ignore or push aside my long-term and short-term emotional issues.

I used to beat up on myself for my lapses. However, I have finally learned that the point of these disciplines is not to do them *perfectly*. That just makes them harder to do. The point is that the more I am able to do them, the better I feel and the better I am able to live out my calling as a minister of the gospel. The less I do them, the less effective I am as one who is called to lead adaptive change in mainline churches.

Perfection is not the point. Yes, Jesus said, "Be perfect...as your heavenly Father is perfect" (Mt. 5:48). But the root word in Greek that is most often translated into English as "perfect" really means "whole." Be whole, even as God is whole. Given that wholeness is related to maturation, the phrase can also be translated, "Be mature as God is mature." This is a challenge more than a judgment—a challenge not to become God, but to be fully human. The more fully human we become, the more fulfilled and useful we are.

The more we pay attention to the personal aspects of adaptive leadership, the more we are able to be the kind of "non-anxious presence" of which Edwin Friedman wrote.

Yet, I confess that during my service in each of five congregations, in middle judicatory ministry, and in denominational ministry, there were times when I became an "anxious non-presence." This is what happens when we become exhausted physically, emotionally, and spiritually. My experience is that exhaustion comes about a little differently in each expression of the church. Your experience may differ from mine, of course, but I suspect one's exhaustion is always related to both one's individual pathologies and to organizational obsolescence.

In congregational ministry, I very much enjoyed being the pastor. It was a privilege to be available to people and to be invited into people's lives at their most vulnerable and tender moments. However, as I moved to larger and larger congregations, I began to tire of the "confinement" of congregational ministry. You couldn't go anywhere "away" without the nagging fear that you would be called back to the parish for some emergency. After twenty some years, when at home, I found myself tensing up whenever the phone rang, afraid that I would be taken away from rest and family to go deal with some emergency, real or imagined. I also spent too many evenings at mind-numbing meetings.

I asked my son, once, "Have you ever thought about ministry as a vocation?" He responded quickly, "No way!"

Taken aback, I asked him why.

He responded, "Because you're never home."

Ouch!

But he was right in his observation. I had been on a neurotic quest to fulfill the dream of my parents' generation of what a really good minister is like. It was a dream that might have been valid in the 1940s, but in the 1980s it had become a nightmare. The demands placed on ministers had multiplied many times between 1940 and 1980, and the context had changed entirely. But most of us were still trying to do ministry the same way. And many of us are *still* trying to do ministry the same way.

Before I left congregational ministry for middle judicatory ministry in 1990, I had figured some of these things out. A sabbatical had brought some deep rest and healing. I had begun to do my congregational ministry in a way that was more sustainable. Feeling better, and seeing so many colleagues around me who were caught in the same trap in which I had been caught, I wanted to help them extricate themselves and to rediscover the joy of congregational ministry. Ironically, it was partly this experience and my sense of mission about it that led me to accept a call to middle judicatory ministry.

Middle judicatory ministry is made for people who love ministers and who love the church as an institution and want to build it up. I quickly and passionately immersed myself in the work of building up congregations and the program of the judicatory itself. I took every occasion to talk with ministers about the importance of tending to their own health and reshaping their ministries and their congregations to fit the new day.

Middle judicatory ministry was great fun in many ways and very satisfying. The hours were long and the driving was particularly hard on the body (50,000 miles a year is a lot of windshield time), but there was seldom the call in the middle of the night. You weren't home a lot, but when you were home, you were really home.

Still, I was doing middle judicatory ministry essentially the same way it had been done for decades before me. Yes, I had a pager, a computer, and a cell phone, but that didn't lower the volume of work, it just sped everything up so you could get more done in your 60–70 hour work week. Of course, by then (the early 1990s) the financial meltdown of the mainline church[3] was well underway, and what had been a middle judicatory staff of several ministers became a two-person staff.

Had I not been called out to go to denominational leadership, I am quite certain that I would either have found a way to do that ministry differently, a way that fit the new context and era, or I would have burned out in just a few years. I like to think I would have found a new way, and I spent much of my next ten years trying to push the thinking about new ways to do ministry in general and in middle judicatory in particular.

I learned a lot of tricks in middle judicatory ministry. For example, I had an index card on my visor that listed every NPR station in Tennessee so I could listen to something edifying while driving. (This was before the days of pod casts and MP3s.) I knew where all the speed traps were. I learned that putting a piece of ice under your tongue can keep you awake for awhile at 1:00 a.m. on a long lonesome stretch of interstate. I learned to call home at night on my cell phone to say good night to my wife and kids.

I remember waking up in the middle of the night once, not knowing where I was. A sense of panic was coming over me as I fumbled around to find a light. Finally, I found a lamp on the bedside table and switched it on, only to discover I was home in my own bed!

Ultimately, middle judicatory work is just hard work, like all ministries. It is made more difficult because the source of your funding is at least one step removed from the pews, so you find yourself getting squeezed harder and harder.

Ministry beyond middle judicatory, in the denominational structures, is hard for many of the same reasons as ministry in middle judicatory. The budget crunch has been a constant struggle for many years. Obsolete organizational forms mean that you end up doing huge amounts of maintenance work that is neither very satisfying nor very productive. But the hardest part is the constant travel.

It is not so much the weariness that comes from driving so many hours, as in middle judicatory ministry. It is hours spent in airline terminals, on overly stuffed planes with worn-out seats that contort your spine. It is the tendonitis you get from schlepping bags through concourses and up into overhead bins. It is the hotels and motels where you are constantly awakened by slamming doors, traveling soccer teams, and by sheer boredom and loneliness. It is all the while trying to keep up with the voice mail and keeping your yet-to-be-answered e-mail messages to no more than 150 or so.

I learned a lot of tricks in denominational ministry. For example, I had a pair of headphones I always carried with me. They didn't go to anything, but when I got on a plane and wanted to work, or it was at the end of a long day or a long trip and I just wanted to sleep or pray or chill, I put the headphones over my ears and stuck the cord in my pocket so that it would look like I was listening to something. That was usually enough to prevent the person next to me from wanting to engage me in conversation. I learned to never, *never* tell your airline seatmate that you are in ministry.

This is all about self-care: intellectual, spiritual, emotional, and physical self-care. Apart from it, one cannot effectively lead adaptive change.

Before Beginning a New Ministry

If you are now or soon to be in the process of seeking a new place of ministry, here is some advice that comes from experience. Getting "started right" in a new ministry, and going in with your eyes wide open, is also an important part of self-care.

1. Engage in a conversation with the search committee about the role of the minister and help them frame (or reframe, if necessary) the role in leadership terms and in a way that makes adaptive change an expectation of them and of you. The committee will need to inform the congregation of this conversation, or they will simply be "setting you up" (and themselves) for a conflict with those members of the congregation that are unaware of these conversations and what they mean. Only so much can be accomplished at this stage, but it is at the very least an opportunity to begin learning essential facts about the congregation and to begin educating folks who may soon be your partners in ministry. It just might result in a more helpful job description.

Even in a very anxious system, the search committee may recognize the need for adaptive change, may be willing to talk about it, and may be attracted to a candidate who can articulate the need for it. Typically, the members of the search committee are chosen from among the brightest and best of the congregation, or of the middle judicatory, or of the denomination that is seeking a new leader. Thus, the members of the search committee are more "ready" than most in an organization. This means they will be the best allies for change, but it also means the rest of the body is not as ready and one must be careful about not pushing too far too fast.

I have always felt that the interview process should benefit the congregation or other institution, whether I got the call or not. They usually spend lots of money to fly you there, put you up, and so forth... but if you use the interview to raise the right questions, they will get their money's worth.

2. If the call comes, and you accept, design a commissioning service rather than an installation service. Use the language of leadership and mission rather than management and maintenance.

3. Resist the temptation to lay blame for what is wrong in the organization. It is especially tempting to blame your immediate predecessor. The assumption is often that the last leader "broke it." But it was probably broken some time ago. It has probably been in the process of becoming "broken" over the past twenty-five years or more. So, it is

doubtful that your immediate predecessor is responsible for all the mess, regardless of his/her level of competence or incompetence. To buy (or sell) the idea that your predecessor "broke it" is to buy (or sell) the idea that *you* can *fix* it; that, my friend, is a thoroughly modern "set up."

I am reminded of Robert Fulghum's marvelous little book, *It Was on Fire When I Lay Down on It.*[4] The book begins:

> A tabloid newspaper carried the story, stating simply that a small-town emergency squad was summoned to a house where smoke was pouring from an upstairs window. The crew broke in and found a man in a smoldering bed. After the man was rescued and the mattress doused, the obvious question was asked: "How did this happen?"
>
> "I don't know. It was on fire when I lay down on it."

In the case of mainline churches, given the perfect storm confronting every expression, you can bet that it isn't simply your predecessor who is responsible for the mess. He or she may have fanned the flames, but it has probably been smoldering for nearly forty years!

4. Don't take it personally when your predecessors blame *you*. I find the mainline church is filled with disappointed retired leaders. Some of them are wonderful people, but many of them left scratching their heads because they couldn't figure out what went wrong.

When I became the Disciples General Minister and President in 1993, one of our regional ministers who was near retirement invited me to accompany him in a drive across his region, stopping in several places to meet local church folks. He was a delightful colleague and it was a marvelous three days. Several times a day we stopped for a reception in a local congregation to meet Disciples from the surrounding congregations. It was a great way to learn about that region and it was a beautiful drive as we passed across mountains and deserts.

In the middle of the journey, we were driving across an open expanse of a couple hundred miles and we had the opportunity to visit in depth with each other. My friend, then in his mid-60s and soon to retire, told me about his call to ministry and the congregations he had served before becoming a regional minister. He spoke of the excitement he had felt in the 1950s and 1960s. He remembered the establishment of the United Nations and the National Council of Churches and the World Council of Churches. The energy rising in his voice, he remembered how the mainline churches were growing by leaps and bounds and how confident he and his colleagues were that they were going to change the world and, in those post–WWII years, win the peace. Even as the separation of church and state was being upheld, they were sure that Christ would be manifest in culture in significant ways. I heard in his voice the echo of the "volunteer establishment" that early Protestant leaders had envisioned for America in its earliest days, but with a social justice that was unknown and unimagined by most of those early American Protestants.

Then, for what seemed like minutes, as he drove along this straight, flat, lonely highway in the middle of nowhere, he stared silently through the windshield, past the desert at the mountains looming in the far distance, replaying in his mind those halcyon days.

Finally, in a somber voice he intoned these poignant words: "It just didn't turn out the way we thought it would."

Those words seem to carry the pain and disappointment of a whole generation. There was no blame, just acknowledgement that it had turned out differently than they had expected.

I feel a special bond with that man to this day. He had experienced it all, beginning to end: the mountaintops of hope and growth, and the valleys of doubt and decline. He blamed no one. He took responsibility for his own naiveté and disillusionment.

But other leaders do not have his grace. Some do not recognize that their assumptions about how the world works erred in some significant ways. For many of them, the pain of that recognition sometimes becomes too much to bear, too much to own as their own responsibility. In their disappointment and grief about how the world failed to meet their expectations and to respond to their leadership as they had believed it would, they sometimes feel the need to lay blame.

This is perfectly understandable. Yet I confess it is always painful when people blame me. I certainly admit to having made mistakes when my turn at leadership came. However, I am not responsible for the "perfect storm" itself.

Perhaps the thing that makes such blaming *exquisitely* painful is that some of these very same colleagues are among those whom I consider my mentors. As a young man, I viewed them from afar with awe and appreciation. They were who I aspired to become. Therefore, it is painful to be criticized by them, explicitly or implicitly, or worst of all, to be *dismissed* by them. I have to talk to myself a lot to remember it is mostly about their disappointments in life and ministry rather than about my own numerous inadequacies as a leader. It is not simply about my inadequacies or their disappointments, but also about my responsibility to critique our denomination, which, like all mainline denominations, had failed yet to respond to the perfect storm in relevant and effective ways. They had expected me to simply "fix" what was broken, to grease the wheels, and get the thing back on the tracks. They failed to understand that those tracks led to a "modern" future that could never come to be.

One must not take these kinds of criticisms personally. It isn't about those of us who are trying to give relevant leadership in the world that *does* exist. We need to have grace for them, just as we will need the grace of those who come after us when they are dealing with the messes we make and with the unfinished business we will necessarily leave behind.

If You Have Been in This Ministry for Some Time...

Most ministers reading this book will do so while having been in a particular ministry for some time. So, it is too late to plan how you will relate to the search committee this go around. However, much of the same conversation will need to take place in an ongoing way with the primary leadership bodies of the institution you are currently serving.

Recognize that the body has become accustomed to your leading in a particular way/style, and seeing you change suddenly can be further anxiety-provoking. You can expect that there will be those who are angered by your change (it will feel like "bait and switch" to them). There will be others who are glad to see the change, but are not sure whether they can trust it.

I call your attention again to Heifetz's example of a pressure cooker. There must be enough heat to facilitate some cooking, but not so much heat that it will blow the lid off! Finding the right balance requires careful monitoring of the membership. A trusted small group that is in touch with the various groups within the organization can be very helpful in regularly taking the temperature of the system and providing regular feedback. Such a group may be an existing leadership group that is already authorized to work with the minister and other leaders in nurturing direction. If there is no such suitable group, it is best to create such a group in consultation with key lay leadership and for the group to be officially authorized by the governing body and provided with a point or points of accountability (so that it does not appear to be merely a group of the primary leaders' "cronies" and, thus, a play for power and control).

When driving, most of us use turn signals when we change direction so as not to surprise those following us. Likewise, it is wise to signal your congregation/institution about changes that are coming in your style and/or approach. Tell the people how you came to see the work differently and why you are seeking to make the changes in approach you feel are needed. Discuss these things with the other primary spiritual leaders of your congregation/institution and invite them to explore with you.

Adaptive change is always provocative. The wise leader is careful to regularly gauge the organization's capacity for more or less "heat." Too much change too fast can lead to destructive chaos. It is seldom appropriate to attempt a frontal assault on the structures of a church system unless trust is very high and there is something of a consensus for change. Rather, work at educating the body to the need for change, while working with those points of health that are present and helping them spread to other parts of the organization. Ministers who have a "two-year plan for complete adaptive change in a church organization" will usually find that the only thing that actually changes is the name of the minister.

I sometimes hear ministers of congregations complain that, in a conflict with a minister, their middle judicatory executive always sides with the congregation. Perhaps this is true in some places. However, my experience as a middle judicatory executive was that ministers were so reticent to ask for help when they needed it that they would instead ride the thing right down to the ground. Then, two feet before crashing, traveling at about a thousand miles an hour, they would call for help. By that time, what is there for the middle judicatory executive to do but try to salvage what's left of a faith community?

Adaptive change is always provocative. Mind the pressure and the temperature.

Systemic Aspects of Leading Adaptive Change

As we think about how to lead adaptive change, one finds there is a sort of an order of work for a transformational leader. This order is not absolute, of course, but depends upon the needs of the individual situation. Neither is the order necessarily linear: you will find yourself jumping and skipping back and forth from one to another. This is part of the challenge of institutions trying to function in postmodern times: things are no longer as linear as they once seemed to be in modern organizations and in the modern context.

Upon analyzing a modern organization, I have heard Loren Mead say, "What we have here is not a 'problem'; what we have is a *mess*." A "problem" suggests a "fix." But a "mess" suggests an intertwining of issues and dynamics that ultimately requires an adaptive response. This is the way it is in institutions today: messy. Instead of a single cultural consensus out of which decisions are made, a cacophony of voices has grown out of generational and racial-ethnic differences. Most mainline churches also face differences among members in their understanding of religious tradition because Christians tend to move across denominational lines more freely than ever before. As people move back and forth from city to suburb to town to exurbia to rural and back again, they have differing assumptions about how congregations should be organized and about the role of the minister and the laity.

Thus, while there is always need for ongoing technical change, we must address the larger picture as well. Otherwise, individual problems will consume all of a leader's time and energy. Still, one cannot ignore technical problems to deal exclusively with adaptive challenges either. It's something like bailing water out of a sinking boat faster and faster without addressing the fact that the hull itself is breaking up and leaking. One cannot simply turn full attention to the adaptive change of building a new hull, lest the boat sink in the meantime. Transformation is *always* a combination of technical and adaptive work done simultaneously and in a continually changing mix.

Leading adaptive change requires some typical elements and patterns. Perhaps you are beginning a new ministry in one or another of the expressions of a mainline tradition (congregation, middle judicatory, or national setting). Or, perhaps you have been in your current ministry for some time and now want to move the institution into adaptive change. In either case, the following elements of leading adaptive change are essential.

1. Understand the context of the institution, both internally and externally.
2. Focus on relationship and trust building.
3. Nurture the faith and spiritual health of the body.
4. Help the body to identify and understand their core values and mission.
5. Identify and address immediately needed technical change.
6. Lead in the development of vision.
7. Nurture the adaptive change that is needed to bring the vision to reality.

1. Understand the Context of the Institution

In his book *Good To Great*, Jim Collins says that successful organizations are, first of all, willing to confront the "brutal facts" that shape their lives and define the challenges of their missions.[1] Part of leadership is exactly this: helping an institution see "the good, the bad, and the ugly" about itself; the functional and dysfunctional; the faithful and unfaithful.

From the standpoint of the leader, failure to do a thorough contextual analysis is dangerous. It is like a novice hunter who gets the sequence wrong: "Ready, fire, aim!" There's no telling who or what might get hit, including the hunter himself.

When working with an organization as a consultant/coach, one of the very first things I do is help the institution get an accurate picture of itself. If a *vision* is a snapshot of what a congregation or other organization will look like after a few years of being and doing what God is calling it to be and do, then the process of *discerning* a vision must begin with a thorough and mutually agreed upon snapshot of what the institution is today. It is the "before" of the "before and after" pictures.

Note I said I *help the institution* get an accurate picture of *itself*. If a consultant or the primary leader (with or without a consultant) simply creates a picture of the congregation as he or she sees it by him- or herself, the power of the picture to clarify and to motivate will be less than if the members of the congregation or other institution participate in the development of the picture for themselves.

Also note that the picture needs to include the good, beautiful, and faithful. While it is important to acknowledge the negative factors, it is the positive factors that will ordinarily motivate people to move forward into God's future for them. This is especially true of people who are attracted to mainline denominations, because a common characteristic of mainline churches is that they tend to focus more on the grace of God than on the judgment of God. But it is also true for *most* people that building on beauty and strength is more attractive than focusing on everything that is wrong and needs to be torn down.

Most dieters find that putting up a picture on the refrigerator of themselves looking their realistic best is more motivating than putting up a picture of themselves looking their worst. One picture helps them accentuate and build on their positive characteristics, while the other picture tends to reinforce their negative self-image and behaviors. The same is true of churches.

On the other hand, some people put up a picture of a favorite movie star or some other incredibly gorgeous image that is *not them,* and that is, frankly, both artificial and unattainable. Like the picture of themselves at their worst, this picture, too, tends to reinforce their negative self-image and behaviors. The same is true of churches.

Thus, working with an existing leadership group, or one that is formed for the purpose, the leader helps create an accurate picture of the institution. In the process leaders will inform both themselves and the institution. This is an in-depth response to the second of the ongoing "Three Most Important Questions"(Conclusion of Part I): Where am I?

What Are the Historical and Social Contexts of This Organization?

When I became the Disciples' regional minister of Tennessee, I quickly discovered that Tennessee is a complicated state. Tennesseans have long referred to the "three states of Tennessee." The state flag has three stars on it, which represent these three very different areas within the state boundaries.

The first is East Tennessee, the land of Davy Crockett and the Appalachian Mountains. This part of the state has its own unique beauty and ethos. Politically, East Tennessee mostly fought for the Union, was against slavery, is today solidly Republican and remains predominantly white. The University of Tennessee is in Knoxville and they are known as "The Volunteers." Geographically, it is comprised of green hills and mountains, including the Great Smokey Mountains (shared with North Carolina). Geography shapes a people, and East Tennesseans are no different from others in this regard.

The hills and hollows tended to isolate settlements of people from one another. An excellent system of roads and interstate highways has long since connected most people and communities to the rest of the state and the nation, but the old ways still live on. There is a certain formality in East Tennessee, and a certain reserve with strangers that befits a people who were not always sure of what a visiting stranger's intentions might have been. Demonstrated character and trustworthiness rates more highly than titles and stated intentions. There is a collective "we'll see" that greets new folks.

But "we'll see" is not the last word. Once you are found to be trustworthy, you will be taken into a community wholly and you will be loyally defended as "all right." Deep friendships form in the midst of this rather severe landscape. Economic prosperity has spread across most of East Tennessee with the rise of the TVA (Tennessee Valley Authority), manufacturing, and the retirement industry. But people are still forming relationships that hark back to the days when a "bad winter" meant depending on the care and generosity of a neighbor to make the difference between a family's life and death.

In contrast, in Middle Tennessee some fought for the Union, some fought for the Confederacy, and most of the area was held and occupied throughout the war by the Union. There were many abuses, hardships, and indignities sustained by the people of Nashville at the hands of Union troops. The gentle green hills made Middle Tennessee the first land in the state west of the Appalachians that was relatively hospitable to farming, railroads, and highways. Thus, Nashville became an important center of commerce as the South grew economically in the twentieth century.

Nashville's recent growth has not been as hot as Atlanta, but it is just as surely New South. People there tend to be generally open to new-comers as "bringers of opportunity." One is reasonably trusted until and unless you demonstrate you are not trustworthy, at which point you are outside the pale. Life tends to be lived at once informally and a little on the opulent side, as tends to be true in much of the New South, partly in cultural memory of the severe shortages in food and other goods suffered during the Civil War. Though perhaps the best known, country music is only one of many industries in the very sophisticated city of Nashville.

Western Tennessee, with its gently rolling landscape gradually flattening out to the Mississippi River, is Old South (though Memphis has begun to show some New South tendencies). Here cotton was king and slavery was the order of the day. Racial attitudes have been slow to change, and enclaves of historic Black culture have produced a rich jazz tradition.

People are genuinely and stereotypically hospitable in Western Tennessee. However, beneath that easy warmth and welcome are a pride and privacy that are not quickly penetrated by people who are "not from here."

In each of these three "states" of Tennessee, there are a thousand variations depending upon whether you are in a small town or a medium or large city; whether the immediate area is primarily farmland or forest; whether the community was shaped by access to a railroad, a highway, a river, or a hunting ground; whether is was settled by a particular religious people or not.

Imagine being a pastor of a congregation and how different your approach might be in the three different areas. Imagine being "regional minister" of such a diverse state. A regional minister in Tennessee must *always* remember where he or she is or risk offending and becoming ineffective. Each area has its beauty and its dignity, and each not only *deserves* to be respected for the best that it represents, but *must* be respected and approached appropriately if ministry is to be done effectively there.

Maybe the place you do ministry is more or less complex than Tennessee. In any case, we need to know and understand our place of ministry. If you are beginning a new ministry, you only get one chance to make a good first impression by approaching people appropriately and with respect for where you and they are. If you missed the opportunity to make that good first impression, it may not be fatal to your ministry, but it may take some remedial relationship building to overcome that poor start. How you lead change in a particular place must always be informed by a deep understanding of where you are and how things work there.

Another tier of questions has to do with the history of your individual institution. Who has been in leadership here before you, how did that go, and why? What have been the major watersheds in the life of the congregation? What are the highlights and low points of the congregation's history?

People who are likely to be able to help answer these kinds of questions include long-time members of the congregation. Of course, everyone sees things from their own perspective, so it is important to hear the congregation's story from more than one person. By visiting for an hour or so with each of six to eight reasonably knowledgeable and healthy people, you can usually piece together a very helpful picture of the institution's history and ethos. As important as an objective and accurate understanding of what has *actually* happened here is the *perception* of history held by key persons.

How are formal and informal power and authority granted, withheld, and utilized in the institution? You know who is on the list of elected officers, but who are the *actual* leaders in the institution? How does change get accomplished or prevented here? How are committees, boards, units held accountable *really* (or are they)? What is the theological "norm" of the congregation? (What do most people in this group believe about God?) How many small groups are there and how much of it is dedicated to governance as opposed to nurture of members and mission?

Every institution is unique. Unless a leader takes the time to consciously and intentionally analyze and think through the uniqueness of how this particular institution functions, it is likely that he or she will stumble across trip wires that trigger explosives, some of which are carefully and deeply hidden. Most of those who comprise the institution know where the trip wires are and assume you do, too. Then, of course, every institution has a few members who are actively engaged in laying the trip wires against you.

The Appendix highlights some of the questions you might ask as you seek to understand your institution's context and as you help the members of the institution understand their own context. I use these kinds of questions as a consultant/coach, but you can use them for your own quest.

As the group completes the research and compiles the answers to these questions, it can begin reviewing the material. Information by itself is not very useful; it is the *meaning* of the information that is important. So, thinking about the content and the implications of the information gathered, the committee begins to "paint" a portrait, a current profile, of the institution. The pastoral leader, or a consultant/coach, or a member of the committee, can draw together an initial draft that puts the information together in a logical way and that draws reasonable inferences and raises appropriate questions about the meaning of the information. But the whole committee must own the final product as fully accurate and reasonably complete. Otherwise, it is merely the "pastor's profile" or the "consultant's profile." To be useful, the whole committee must own it. Using consensus, it is a matter of painting as complete a portrait as the committee can agree upon. Points of disagreement should also be identified so that others reading the profile may know some of the questions that were asked but about which the committee could not arrive at common conclusions.

Time spent in getting an accurate sense of the historical, social, and personal context of the institution will be time well spent as you begin a new ministry or as you begin to lead adaptive change. People will appreciate and honor your efforts to understand and will gladly help "educate" you for your and their mutual benefit.

2. Focus on Relationship and Trust Building

Relationship and trust are two of the fundamental building blocks of health in any institution. Members must be able to trust their leaders and one another.

For leaders, this means being genuine and operating with integrity. It means being present to people in a way that demonstrates care. It means keeping confidences and providing safe places within the organization for people to share individually and in groups. It means making sure that effective communication is taking place within the body so that no one has the sense that decisions are being made secretly, or without reasonable input from the larger body. It is not enough to offer people the opportunity to comment, ways must be found to *actively* solicit people's comments and thoughts.

In a congregation where there has been a major breach of trust by a leader, particularly a breach of ethics, a new leader will find it more difficult to earn that trust. Sometimes this mistrust will be expressed in open hostility and sometimes it will be expressed in a kind of passive resistance. In either case, it behooves the leader to spend extra time and energy in trust building.

Often when there has been a major conflict or a breach of ethics, the lay leadership of a congregation will try to get the discomfort over with as soon as possible. Typically, this means these matters never get aired to the congregation openly and honestly but are instead handled "quietly" by a few key leaders. This comes across to the wider congregation as "sweeping the matter under the rug" and further undercuts trust. Except as it may hurt innocent individuals, it is much better and healthier for leaders to fully disclose what happened and what response was made. Trying to "play it close to the vest" will ultimately serve no one's best interests. There may yet be those who try to Monday-morning-quarterback the course of action taken by the leadership, but a nondefensive, "we did the best we knew to do after prayer and consultation" will generally suffice.

If there was not full disclosure at the time of the conflict, the best course of action for a new leader may be to research what actually happened and to sensitively but fully share the story with the wider body (better late than never). Such a disclosure must never be made, however, in a way that makes it appear as though the congregation's lay leadership or the new leader is being vindictive or self-serving. It is perhaps better for the new leader to lead the group in disclosing it for themselves rather than the new leader being the point person.

As a rule, whenever a mainline church has a conflict or a key leader engages in unethical behavior, the faster the middle judicatory executive can be brought into the situation, the better. Most have experience in dealing with these kinds of issues and some measure of authority to do so.

When congregations have a fight, it often leaves deep wounds that require attention. If the congregation does not effectively deal with the fallout generated by a fight, there will usually be one of two outcomes:

either the congregation will continue in open conflict (usually finding new things to fight over) or the congregation will become passive. What results, open conflict or passivity, may depend on the personalities of the primary leaders and how open they are to resolution on the one hand or how open they are to honest discussion of differences on the other. Some congregations have been fighting so long that no one remembers what the original issue was!

In the course of resolution, some may leave the congregation because they find they are just not able to get over their hurt. These people should be helped to leave with dignity and love and not to be treated as a case of "good riddance." This is important both for their personal state of mind and spirit and for going out into the wider community to "process" any sense of having been pushed out unfairly. The pastor must be able to put such a departure in perspective and not regard it as a personal failure on his or her part (unless it is, of course; in which case the pastor will need to seek grace from God and from both the congregation and from him- or herself.)

It is wise to invite in a middle judicatory leader or a competent consultant to help a congregation work through long-standing issues and the fallout they generate in the form of broken relationships and mistrust. There are also liturgical resources for helping congregations work through old wounds.

The bottom line is this: leading adaptive change is not possible unless the leader has the relationships and perceived trustworthiness necessary. Likewise, a congregation or other institution cannot be led into adaptive change if there is not sufficient trust between the members themselves.

3. Nurture the Faith and Spiritual Health of the Body

There is a deep longing among so many contemporary Americans for a sense of connection with that which is the source of life and meaning (what Paul Tillich called "the Ground of Being"). This longing is a normal human experience because we were created with an innate need for connection with our Creator. Even many who are not religious in the usual sense of the word long for and seek this connection with the Source.

Contemporary life, with its hurriedness and "harriedness," leaves us all with a sense of disconnection. The great American Quaker Elton Trueblood, was right in speaking of us as a "cut-flower civilization."[2] A cut-flower civilization, as Trueblood explained it, is one that is cut off from its roots, one that has no means by which to draw nurture and sustenance from its soil. This painfully describes most of us who live in this secular era of lightning-fast change. Because of the geographic and socioeconomic mobility typical of so many of us today, we feel cut off from our origins (some of us have *deliberately* cut ourselves off from our origins), from that which launched us in life. We often feel like "dry bones" living in a desert land.[3]

"Who and what are we?" This is perhaps *the* question of the current age. Most of the old signposts that used to tell us who we are have been taken down or are rotted away, covered by moss, or point to irrelevant destinations. Since 1920, but especially since 1968 (the beginning of the postmodern era), traditional authorities of all kinds have been mostly disregarded or found wanting, and thus discounted and rejected. This disintegration of authority has occurred in the midst of the assassinations of the 1960s; the exposure of the hypocrisy of White America through the civil rights movement; desegregation; the Vietnam experience; Watergate; "Irangate"; "Monicagate"; the fall of several televangelists; the cultural disestablishment of the mainline church; the disintegration of the extended and nuclear family; the advent of mass communication; the rise of relativism; and all the rest of the public and private traumas, shifts, and systemic dismantling of institutions and traditions we have experienced. We have seen nothing less than the unraveling of modern society, along with its faith in inevitable progress and the fundamental goodness of humankind. No wonder we are confused.

In the face of the unraveling of the modern era, we have taken to calling this the *postmodern era*. But the term "postmodern" itself reveals our confusion. We do not know *what* this era is, we just know it is no longer the modern era. It is a period of transition, that is for certain; but we do not know if it will last for decades or for centuries, and we do not know what we are transitioning *to*. Wave after wave of change has left us stunned and disoriented.

In the face of the confusion and powerlessness we often feel in contemporary life, no wonder there have arisen so many "spiritualities." Many of these are explicitly or implicitly unchristian. Our culture and the mainline churches are in spiritual crisis. Because the mainline churches have done so little to nurture faith and the life of the Spirit in recent decades, many of our members are ill-equipped to live in Christian purpose and confidence.

Some readers will incorrectly assume that "adaptive change" means simply adapting to the current cultural norms of the larger society. But there is no reason for mainline churches to continue, let alone to grow in numbers or effectiveness, if they simply seek to accommodate culture. Those distinctive core values that are at the heart of what mainline churches represent at their best must be recovered, reaffirmed, re-grounded, and maintained and strengthened even as adaptive change is undertaken.

Some of those core values, such as "holding faith and reason together," were communicated and reinforced by "mainline culture" itself. But after 1968, the culture did not promulgate this core, along with others. This means that today, if such values are to be learned, they must be taught with intentionality.

Few members of the mainline churches are familiar with John Wesley's Quadrilateral, though it is at the heart of the mainline churches' approach to spiritual truth. The Quadrilateral holds that there are four primary sources of understanding God's self-revelation: Scripture, reason, faith, and tradition (the church's own memory and history).[4] Because fundamentalism is so powerfully present in the culture today, three of the Quadrilateral's sources are ignored and members of mainline churches easily fall prey to biblical literalism. Unfortunately, Christian education in mainline churches has been in decline for decades. As a result, members of mainline churches are woefully unfamiliar with the contents of the Bible, with the spiritual disciplines, and with the history of the wider church and of their own denominational tradition.

A consequence of this ignorance is that members of mainline churches become "easy pickings" for more reactionary, fundamentalist traditions that do not seek to hold faith and reason together. At the same time, they become more susceptible to theological assumptions that are essentially non-Christian and that cannot stand in the face of what we know about the world today.

Effective Christian education goes beyond "knowledge." It also involves praxis: mainline churches must provide opportunities for putting faith and knowledge into action lest members' faith be unsustainable in the current era.

Thus "adaptive change" means more than simply adapting current modes of operation in order to accommodate culture. It means adapting to modes of operation that are both sustainable *and* that exhibit the capacity to transform persons and culture.

The good news of cultural disestablishment is that the mainline churches can no longer depend on mainline culture to communicate their core values and mission. This is good news because, so long as the mainline churches depended upon mainline culture in this way, the culture also had a way of distorting and contaminating those core values and that mission. The bad news is that such "freedom" from dependence on the culture does not automatically result in the effective communication of core values and mission or in effective transformative ministry. It is therefore necessary to seek adaptive change that enables the church to utilize methodologies that function effectively in current culture idioms while teaching Christians how to live a life of faithfulness in such an era, providing opportunities for living out such faithfulness.

We must teach the spiritual disciplines and lead in them, providing various opportunities for people at various levels of readiness. Some people need instruction, some need formal structures to assist them in their disciplines (such as prayer services, study groups), and some need only encouragement. But all need to see faith and spiritual health lived and modeled intentionally by their leaders.

4. Help the Body to Identify and Understand the Core Values and Mission

In the face of the incredibly rapid social change we have witnessed since 1968, all mainline denominations have drifted somewhat in our understanding of our identity and our mission. We have become confused about who and what God is calling us to be. It is not only mainline denominations as a whole that need greater clarity about their identity and mission. Congregations and middle judicatories have drifted in their sense of purpose. My experience as a congregational minister, a middle judicatory minister, and a head of communion suggests that a primary key to vitality is a clear sense of identity and mission that is related to the cultural and geographical context in which the ministry is situated. It is past time for us to consider anew what our mission is in this land, especially in the face of our diminished resources and in the face of our cultural disestablishment and loss of influence. Who are we called to be *now* and what are we called to do *now*? It is urgent that we gain clarity in these matters.

In the absence of such clarity, and in the face of the declines in numbers of members and dollars, we have tended to focus on survival. But such a focus will kill a church.

The lifeblood of the church is mission. God calls the church to pour itself out in mission. Jesus' words apply to institutions as much as to individuals, "Those who want to save their life will lose it, and those who lose their life for my sake shall find it." (Lk. 9:24) When the church becomes anxious and turns in on itself, it loses its identity as the body of Christ and a miserable life is followed by a usually miserable death. How does a leader address these matters?

A number of approaches are available. First, if you are in a call system that requires candidates to interview with a committee, questions about the identity, core values, and mission of the organization should be on your primary list of questions to ask the search committee. If they don't have an answer, you may still accept a call to that ministry, but their inability to state the mission clearly is important information for you to have as you plan your work among them. Also, I have always viewed an interview with a search committee as being itself a ministry to the organization. If they do not realize they are without a clear sense of identity, core values, and mission, they should know it once they have interviewed you and been interviewed by you.

Once you are in the role of leader, you can help the church move forward through teaching, preaching, and writing. It is partly a matter of institutional self-discovery and partly a matter of a leader educating the members of the institution. A leader should never assume that the institution either remembers or understands its own history or its connections to the church beyond itself. As General Minister and President of the Disciples of Christ, I used every available opportunity to ask questions and to talk and write about our identity, our core values, and our mission: in my state of the church address to our biennial general assembly, in my addresses to gatherings of denominational and middle judicatory leaders, in my sermons and addresses to regional assemblies, in magazine articles and pastoral letters to the church, in video presentations, and in my frequent preaching in congregations and other settings.

There is seldom a person who has more authority or responsibility to address this issue with the organization than the senior minister, the middle judicatory executive, or the chief denominational executive. People *expect* these senior leaders to address the mission and purpose of the organization they lead. If *no one* is addressing the mission and purpose of the organization, a spiritually debilitating malaise sets in. If anyone *other than* the senior leader is leading the charge in doing so, it is likely a prelude to serious conflict because the senior leader will be seen as not doing his or her job.

Having said this, the mission or purpose cannot simply be *proclaimed* by the senior leader. The leader needs to lead the body in *discerning* it. In a congregation, that probably means taking it up with the senior lay leaders while the rest of the congregation is encouraged to overhear the conversation and has meaningful opportunity to comment. In a middle judicatory, it probably means appointing a "blue ribbon" representative group to work through to a clear statement that is then tested with the larger body of leadership. In a denomination, well, I appointed a panel of scholars and church leaders to help us think about these things. It was in my first year of service as GMP, so it was too early to cast a vision, but the group did an excellent job of naming our identity and core values, an important first step. These were then discussed among as many groups of denominational, middle judicatory, and congregational leaders as possible as well as by the denominational board, which was responsible for ultimately affirming them. The point is not simply to create long lists of values and a catchy mission statement. The point is to create ownership and to help people internalize the information and think about the implications for the way the organization does its work.

The Mission of the Congregation

God always calls a congregation to a mission that is both rooted in the mission of the whole body of Christ and that is expressed in an interplay of the congregation's gifts with the needs found in the congregation's locale. So, there are three things leaders need to help their congregation understand: the mission of the whole body of Christ, their own gifts as a congregation, and the needs of those in their immediate locale.

The challenge may be in identifying and owning an immediate locale. Some congregations are committed to serving a locale that no longer exists. That is, they are still offering what people who no longer live there needed. Thus an Anglo congregation that was established in a neighborhood that was originally Anglo but that has become a predominantly Hispanic neighborhood has a challenge. This congregation will need to decide either to serve the new people living in the original locale or they will need to decide to serve a new locale. In the case of a neighborhood church, the congregation that stays in touch with its changing neighborhood will be able to change along with the neighborhood. But the longer an established congregation goes without staying in touch with its neighborhood, the less likely it is going to be able to succeed in addressing the neighborhood's new needs (no matter how sincerely they may wish to do so). Such a congregation may have little choice but to close, to physically move to a new location, or to seek to meet the needs of a locale within which the building is not situated. It has become contextually obsolete and irrelevant. The sooner the situation is recognized and addressed, the more likely the congregation can return to health.

Missionaries in a foreign land learn the language and get to know the people they are to reach and serve so they will know how to go about their work. When a congregation does not speak the language (literally or figuratively) of the people in the target area, having little or no clue as to who the people living there really are, it is not surprising to find resistance, failure, and disappointment. Such congregations, focused inwardly, as they usually are, will typically blame *those people* who moved into the neighborhood over the years. They will often claim that they are a welcoming congregation but *"those people* just aren't interested in church." Bigoted statements may often be heard. They may also refuse to take responsibility for their gifts, which could be used in a mission to that target area. In contrast, a congregation focused on mission, instead of on themselves, is going to reach out into the community and meet *those people* where they are or choose another target area they are willing to serve. The sooner they do one or the other the better, and the senior leader has a responsibility to lead the church in a process of clarification and discernment of identity, core values, and mission.

Can a congregation be faithful and yet choose to serve a target area or areas beyond the location of their building? I believe it is possible. However, it depends upon the individual congregation, its discernment, and its circumstances as to whether they actually *are* being faithful or are actually running away from the calling God has given them. I don't think any congregation should ever dare to become completely *comfortable* with a decision to serve elsewhere.

The Mission of Middle Judicatories and National Denominational Organizations

Denominational structures have served many purposes through the last two centuries in America. In the nineteenth century, denominations were focusing primarily on starting new congregations and developing leadership. By the late nineteenth century, the facilitation of mission overseas had become another primary role. In the 1960s, in the face of the civil rights struggle and the Vietnam War, witnessing for social justice became a core role of denominational structures (social justice had long been on denominational agendas, but it now took on a more central role.)

By the 1980s, in the face of decline, denominational structures became more and more preoccupied with maintenance and survival issues (especially that of the individual denominational units themselves rather than that of the congregations or the whole denomination). Though such activity was usually couched in mission and "whole church" terms, primary energy was given to defining a sustainable niche for the individual denominational units themselves, trying to make their own unit indispensable and economically "bullet-proof," rather than really addressing the health of the larger body.

Without a clarification of the mission of American denominations in the face of the church's changed relationship to the culture, denominational structures will continue to be driven by their own maintenance and survival rather than by a relevant sense of mission. This manifests itself in an effort on the part of individual denominational units (middle and national) to become *hubs of control* (the default "modern" role) rather than *hubs of communication and networking* (the default "postmodern" role). There is a precise correlation between individual denominational units being "hubs of control" and the rise of parachurch organizations that operate as "hubs of communication and networking."

Adaptive change is made all the more difficult in middle judicatory and denominational structures because (1) most have been structured in a way that makes change very difficult; and (2) by their very distance from the pew, it is more difficult to hold middle and national organizational structures accountable to the membership for needed ongoing change (unlike in the congregation where members have contact with each other and with their leaders weekly or daily, most members have little contact with middle judicatory and denominational leadership and little understanding of the mission of those organizations).[5]

There are three primary focuses for the faithful middle judicatory. The first is to help congregations be faithful and effective instruments of mission *where they are.* This will mean providing some services directly to congregations and, increasingly, networking and brokering other services.

The second primary focus for the middle judicatory is to help congregations faithfully extend their mission *beyond* where they are. So, the middle judicatory helps the congregation extend its ministry across the geographic area of the middle judicatory. This might be accomplished, for example, by facilitating the starting of new congregations and the revitalization of existing congregations, and by providing camps and conferences and other youth programs that provide something more than individual congregations can provide by themselves, or by helping congregations address justice issues.

The third primary focus for the middle judicatory is connecting congregations to the wider church, broadening their identity and extending their mission to the whole world. The middle judicatory is thus important connecting tissue in the body of Christ.

This means that middle judicatory leaders and their boards need to ask three primary evaluative questions: (1) Are we helping congregations be more effective in their local mission? (2) Are we effectively helping congregations to extend their mission into the whole geographic area served by this middle judicatory? (3) Are we effectively connecting congregations to the wider church, broadening their identity and extending their mission into the whole world?

For faithful national units there are related primary focuses, depending upon the purpose of the unit. First, for units whose purpose is to be engaged in overseas ministries, higher education, and domestic mission programming, the primary focus is helping congregations extend their ministry beyond their middle judicatory's geography to the whole nation and around the world. It is easier, and more in keeping with the pre-1968 world, for these units to work in a way that says, "We of this national unit have an important mission which you, as congregations, should fund." But the more faithful and relevant stance is, "We of this national unit have an important means by which you as congregations can extend *your* mission to the whole nation and around the globe." The difference is subtle, but powerful.

Second, for units whose purpose is to provide services for congregations, the primary focus is providing real, effective services to congregations. These services will be provided either directly or through brokering and networking in partnership with middle judicatories and with resources outside the denomination itself.

Thus, there are two primary evaluative questions that national unit leaders and their boards need to ask: (1) "Are we effectively providing services to congregations in ways that help them to be more effective in fulfilling their mission locally?" (2) "Are we effectively connecting congregations to the wider church, broadening their identity and extending their mission into the whole world?"

The wise leader, whether in the setting of a congregation, a middle judicatory, or a national unit, will understand that "connection" to the wider body and the world is nothing less than *countercultural.* It isn't countercultural in the sense of being over against postmodern culture, which takes global connection for granted. *But it is countercultural in terms of the* **modern** *organizational culture that still pervades mainline denominations.*

Modern approaches tend to create silos, to build up autonomies, and to imagine self-sufficiencies. *Postmodern* approaches realize that *disconnection is death.*

5. Do Technical Change as Needed

As has been said, when it comes to change, it is not that technical change is bad and adaptive change is good. Both have their place. It is a matter of engaging in each as needed. The problem is when institutions engage in *only* technical change, or substitute technical for adaptive change.

It is often necessary to engage in some technical change before adaptive change is possible. In the medical example we used before, when a person is having severe chest pains, that is not the time for contemplating a major change in one's lifestyle. It is time to get to the hospital as quickly as possible, because a technical "fix" is called for. After the bypass or angioplasty is done, then is the time to think about why the arteries got stopped up to begin with and to think about what adaptive changes you need to make in lifestyle to restore health to your cardio-vascular system.

Sometimes technical change is necessary in order to make adaptive change possible. For example, say in your congregation of five hundred active members you have one of those seventy-five member boards with a rate of attendance around 20 percent each meeting. It is desirable to make an adaptive change by downsizing the board and changing its role. However, because the board has had such low attendance, there is not enough trust within the system to make such a change possible. People will think someone is trying to grab for power. So, in this case, you engage in technical change first by doing everything possible to crank up the system as it currently exists. Extra announcements are made from the pulpit, perhaps postcards are sent to board members, or each member is phoned to remind them of the meetings: all to get the system back on its feet so enough trust will be built eventually to make it possible to implement the desired change to a smaller board that functions in a new way. Initially, it requires a high output of energy, but it eventuates in the possibility of a new model that functions more effectively and requires less of the leadership's time and energy.

As one thinks about relationships, programs, and management, the better shape these are in, the lower the anxiety in the system, and the easier it is to do adaptive change (provided the need for the adaptive change has been made clear). This is one reason why it is better to build on strengths than to try to motivate people by magnifying the weaknesses of the organization. Dwelling on weaknesses and failures raises anxiety and thus raises resistance to change. Building on strengths lowers anxieties and, in turn, lowers the kind of resistance that is fueled by anxiety.

6. Lead in the Development of Vision

To paraphrase the proverb, "Without a vision, the institution perishes." A vision, if adequately related to the mission and to the actual context (both internal and external) can create and release new spiritual energy.

Leading in the development of a vision is not the same as simply "making up" a vision and pushing it on the membership. Leading in the development of vision means nurturing healthy organizational dynamics and providing processes that enable people to trust, dream, and discern. The leader may well participate in the discernment of a collective vision by naming some elements he or she sees, but it is fundamentally a group process.

Creating a vision statement is not the same thing as *having vision* or *discerning a vision*. "Creating a vision statement" is something that secular organizations do as a function of strategic planning. It is appropriate for secular organizations to do visioning that way because God is not part of the process. But in the church, a real vision comes through the Holy Spirit, not through a committee pulled together to figure out on their own what the church "ought" to do or what they want the church to do.

So, a visioning committee's work is (1) to provide a process of discernment that involves the whole membership; (2) to gather or harvest the elements of vision that are received by various members of the congregation out of the process; and (3) to craft those elements into a statement, or a story, or a "picture" of what the congregation will look like in a few years if it becomes and does what God is calling it to be and to do now. In the end, the committee holds that picture up to the congregation and asks, "Is this a reasonable representation of the picture you are getting from the Holy Spirit?" Or, "How can this picture be changed to reflect what you discern God is calling us to become?" In this way, the congregation arrives together at an inspired understanding of the direction God is calling it to go in the transformational journey.

If the "before" picture is the one created through a realistic assessment of where the congregation is now, a *vision* is an "after" picture, a kind of a snapshot of what the church will look like after it has for a few years been being and doing what God is calling it to be and do. Actually, I think of this picture as more of a "watercolor" than a photograph or an oil painting. The edges are a little fuzzy and this color runs into that color a bit so that the picture is not precise…and yet it is provocative and clear enough to give direction and to generate energy. It is, as my partner George Bullard would say, a "future story." But the story is not woven so tightly that there is no room for further discernment or creativity.

A carefully discerned and stated vision provides a "big picture." In the absence of a *big* picture, the individual cells of the organization (individual congregations, middle judicatory bodies, or denominational programmatic units, etc.) will tend to create their own smaller visions. These may serve to build up the strength of that individual cell, but without really strengthening the whole body (even though their individual vision statements will almost always be made to *sound* like they are serving the whole body). The larger body may end up looking like Popeye, with grossly over-developed arms and scrawny legs (and no spinach to miraculously make them work together as needed).

Returning to the three elements of the visioning committee's work, what might a process of discernment that involves the whole membership look like? It will begin by assessing the current state of the congregation or, if that has recently been done satisfactorily, lifting that assessment up to the congregation so they can see themselves as they are. It will then offer a process that involves significant numbers of the members in disciplined prayer for vision. This is difficult for most mainline churches. Why?

It is difficult because most of us are not used to praying together, out loud, listening to one another's hearts. We typically feel the need to rush in and fix something rather than finding joy in simply "being who we are before God and before each other." We are accustomed to having someone *pray on our behalf as a group* as in the pastoral prayer on Sunday morning or before a Sunday school class perhaps. Yet actually praying with and for one another and for the church *out loud* is unusual. However, it is a practice from which we could benefit greatly. It is a practice that *requires* practice.

I commend to you a process developed by George Bullard called "prayer and share triplets." It calls for groups of three persons each to meet together for prayer ten times, for one hundred minutes over the course of one hundred days. You can find details of this approach in *Pursuing the Full Kingdom Potential of Your Congregation* (St. Louis: Lake Hickory Resources, 2005) or at www.TheColumbiaPartnership.org.

Not every mainline congregation, or every mainline member, will find this approach fits their needs. However, I believe every discernment process should provide for actual *praying* as well as reflection. Otherwise, the process may simply be a function of the head and finally be no different than any ordinary strategic planning process that so many of us have done so many times before—a process that does not really invite the Holy Spirit in.

The glimpses of vision that are gotten in these prayer groups then need to be harvested and shared with the congregation. This sharing may be accomplished on Sunday mornings during the pastoral prayer time, or at another time in worship, or in the newsletter, or otherwise made available to the congregation. Once these are gathered, the group responsible for the visioning process reviews them and begins putting together a collective vision, which is then reviewed, tested, and amended until it is affirmed by the congregation. This congregational affirmation is best done through the development of consensus, rather than by "debate and vote." The vision should then remain a working document, open for new insights and direction from the Spirit.

7. Lead the Work That Will Help Bring the Vision About

Once the congregation has received and affirmed the vision, a strategic plan can be put together either by the group responsible for the visioning or by another group designated for the purpose. The vision will be the guiding star for all planning. If the visioning committee is not charged with the development of the plans, then members of that group should probably be involved in the planning processes so as to help keep the vision front and center. The plan will need to clearly address both technical and adaptive change, and will provide the programmatic "legs" needed to begin nurturing the vision into reality. The plan will also provide for accountability; that is, holding the organization, its leadership, and members *accountable* to the change they committed themselves to making, to the mission they committed to serve, and to the vision they committed to follow.

Because the need for adaptive change is ongoing (since the context as well as the institution itself are constantly changing), the useful life of a vision is typically only a few years. Adaptive leaders will want to help the organization revisit the vision regularly, to see if the vision is still relevant in every respect or whether some refreshing of the vision is needed. In any case, about every five-to-seven years it is time to undergo another full-blown visioning process to be sure that the caravan keeps moving, and in the right direction.

This five- to seven-year cycle of revisioning corresponds to the typical five-to-seven-year cycle I see in ministry itself. A new minister arrives and spends a year or two getting familiar with the people, the institution, and the context. The next three to four years are spent initiating new ideas and approaches. The last year or two of the cycle are spent consolidating that which has been implemented. Then, the minister either leaves (too frequently the case) or a new cycle of ministry begins in the same institution. If a sabbatical is available to the minister when a cycle of ministry is in the beginning of the consolidation phase, that time away can be used by the minister to reflect upon the next cycle of ministry in that place rather than becoming a time to think about where he or she will move next. Without a sabbatical, a minister is likely to encounter burnout and will move simply to escape the discomfort of the experience.

There are yet two questions that need to be addressed.

The first is, "Why bother?" If leading adaptive change in mainline churches is such hard work, wouldn't it just be better to let the mainline churches die and start over with a clean slate?

The second question is, "How can we move forward in hope?" If God does not want us to simply fade away, what *is* God calling us to be and do in this postmodern era?

Why Bother?

The institutional decline we have witnessed since 1968 in mainline denominations would not be particularly troubling if these bodies had no important contribution to make to the faithfulness and effectiveness of their congregations and to the whole body of Christ. However, I believe these denominations (or *some* similar connective structures) *do* have an important role to play in the health of the church of Jesus Christ. The mainline denominations were created in large measure to provide important support for faithful and effective congregational life and mission that would reach into the local context *and* into the whole world. The trouble began, in part, when denominational bureaucrats began to think that congregations were created primarily to provide financial support for denominational structures.

"Denomination" means something very different in regard to mainline churches today than it did two hundred years ago. In the nineteenth century, the mainline denominations and their predecessors were highly sectarian. While these denominations shared a common vision of a Protestant America and cooperated in some ways to bring it about, each also understood *itself* to be in some sense the *most* or *only* faithful embodiment of the gospel of Jesus Christ.

In contrast, today these denominations and their successor bodies are engaged together in a multitude of ecumenical expressions, works, and dialogues with each other and beyond themselves. Though particular forms and practices continue to differ in significant ways from one mainline denomination to another, each recognizes the others' ministries and each feels free to share in the others' celebrations of the Lord's Supper. While each, no doubt, feels most comfortable "in their own clothes," no one believes their own denomination to be the *most* or *only* faithful embodiment of the gospel. All mainline heads of communions (and most other mainline church leaders, including those of congregations and middle judicatories) would make the case that each tradition brings its own gifts to the mix of American Christianity and helps to balance the expressions and excesses of each other's individual communion.

While denominations *can* be and *sometimes are* self-serving and counterproductive, especially when they succumb to the temptation to become ends in themselves, they are still valuable structures within American Christianity for which a suitable substitute has yet to be found.

Why are they "valuable structures"? They are valuable because of their core purposes and the core values that yet drive them in significant ways. I believe there are three core purposes of mainline denominations. First, these denominations help congregations do together what can *only* be done, or can *best* be done, together. Few congregations can muster the resources necessary to generate a summer camp and conference program for children and youth. Even if a congregation has the resources, the resulting program will not have the benefit of their children and youth interacting with those of other congregations, some of whom will be from *very* different social and/or racial ethnic backgrounds. Few congregations can create their own accredited graduate level theological education. Few congregations can create a health care insurance program for their employees. Few congregations can generate a domestic and overseas mission program that truly "goes into all the world."

Second, denominations nurture a particular *ethos*. "Ethos" refers to the way we do things as a church: how we worship, how we govern ourselves, what we think is most important and what we think is unimportant, how we decorate and do not decorate our buildings, what we call things, our characteristic attitudes. In short, our ethos is *who we are as a church family expressed in how we do things and how we think about things.* One church family's ways of doing things are not intrinsically better than the way another church family does them, but they do have a certain consistency and integrity. Being United Methodist or Disciples of Christ is not better in any ultimate sense than being Presbyterian or, for that matter, Roman Catholic or Church of the Nazarene. But each has its own ways of doing things and we each have to express ourselves as church by some consistent ethos or our church life is chaotic, confused, and conflicted. By recognizing that all our various denominational families are part of the One Family of Jesus Christ, the church universal, and by honoring one another and working together, we can learn from one another, help correct each other's excesses, and help each see their own blind spots and weaknesses.

Third, denominations provide for mutual accountability. As individuals, each of us needs to be personally accountable to someone. Our congregations and the other institutions and structures of our denominations need accountability also. Every church leader (lay or clergy) knows there are crazy members, crazy ministers, and unhealthy congregations. Every system has to provide a way for these people and organizations to be held accountable lest they destroy individuals and congregations.

Ultimately, of course, we are all accountable to Jesus Christ. But few of us are capable of completely understanding Christ's will in every situation. Our own agendas and prejudices enter into the picture, and so we often do not recognize or discern what it is Christ would have us do. Sometimes we incorrectly identify our own strongly held desires and opinions as those of Jesus Christ. This is just part of being human, and so we need someone beyond ourselves to help keep us "honest" with ourselves and with Jesus Christ. Thus we look to our denominations as a source of collective wisdom and discernment—as a "reality check." Of course, our denominations do not always have the answers right either, but they do help keep the right questions before us and provide alternative perspectives.

No one can be the body of Christ by himself or herself. No one is an island, no congregation is an island, and not even a denomination is an island. Each is a part, and only a part, of the whole body of Christ. Each part needs every other part, because this is the very essence of the church God called into being and because we need the other parts to keep us honest. We are accountable to God through Christ's *whole* body, the *whole* church. Denominations then, *when they are functioning properly,* hold all the individuals and institutions within them accountable to each other and to Christ. Denominational structures are themselves held accountable by their own members, by their own structures, and by their fellowship and in working together with other denominations.

The mainline denominations are "valuable structures" also because of the core values they represent. These core values are particularly important in the midst of an era in which Americans are consumed with anxiety, much religion wraps itself in the flag, patriotism daily crosses over the line into nationalism, fundamentalism is on the rise around the world, and our government seems bent on justifying American Empire in evangelical terms. Here, then, are five reasons why the core values of mainline denominations are especially important today.

First, in a time when fundamentalism is sweeping all the religions of the world, it is valuable to have traditions that seek to *hold faith and reason together.* While we have seen fundamentalism creeping even into many mainline institutions, authentic mainline denominational traditions all maintain that *faith and reason do belong together.* This is an important core value that is worth keeping before twenty-first–century Americans.

Second, and related, the colleges, seminaries, and universities rooted in the mainline denominations are engaged in education rather than indoctrination.[1] At a time when much that passes for education is really mere indoctrination within a context of moral and religious authoritarianism, or mere passing of technocratic information in a context of moral and religious sterility, mainline churches still celebrate and support *liberal arts education*.[2]

Third, the mainline denominations represent a worldview that *analyzes reality both in terms of individuals and systems*. This is a particularly important corrective to an American ethos of radical individualism that tends to see good and evil only in individual terms. Any truly biblical notion of justice must appreciate the systemic nature of evil as well as the individual's propensity toward sin. Furthermore, at its best, mainline Christian theology is self-critical and teaches the need for all systems to be self-critical (including the American national system itself).

Fourth, it is mainline theology and biblical interpretation that has made it possible for *women, people of color, and other historically marginalized people to participate more fully* in the church and in the wider community (though this is certainly a work in progress both in and beyond the church).

Fifth, the mainline churches exemplify overseas involvements that are marked by *partnership with indigenous people rather than by colonialism*. Mainline theology helps us differentiate between the United States and the authentic reign of God. This is an important witness to America and the world.

It has and will be argued, of course, that all of the demonic approaches above (the separation of faith and reason, indoctrination, extreme individualism, marginalization of certain people, and colonialism) have been hallmarks of the mainline church in the past and, of course, that there remain elements of these in mainline church life and practice. Nevertheless, any authentic mainline witness does not support these things today.

Five Reasons Why Mainline Denominations Are "Valuable Structures"

1. They hold *faith* and *reason* together at a time when the world seems bent on separating the two.
2. Their institutions of higher education engage in *education* rather than *indoctrination*.
3. They have a worldview that *analyzes reality both in terms of individuals and systems,* rather than through the lens of radical individualism only.
4. They interpret the Scriptures in a way that *empowers women, people of color, and other historically marginalized people to participate more fully* in the church and the wider culture.
5. Their overseas involvements are marked by partnership with indigenous people rather than by colonialist approaches.

Before consenting (or even rejoicing) in the "killing off" of mainline denominations, we must ask, what will stand in the cultural breach resulting? Certainly there are other authentic and effective voices within the American Christian scene, including, for example, those of the historic African American communions, the historic peace churches, and those of socially aware evangelicals. But do any of these have the institutional potential of the mainline denominations, which, even in their weakened state, have more than thirty million members?

Until such time as an effective alternative embodiment of these values can be developed, it is important to help the mainline denominations find greater health, and not just denominational structures, but the congregations they serve. The seeds of the development of such an "effective alternative embodiment" are among us in the form of the fruits of current and past ecumenical dialogues and newly developing ecumenical relationships and working partnerships for the sake of mission. Yet these remain only seeds that can hardly stand up to the harsh climate of the postmodern world.

Therefore, I would make the case that mainline denominations must not be *replaced* so much as *reinvented*. This reinvention will necessarily involve a partnership between the local, middle, and national leadership and must also be undertaken in conversation with ecumenical partners and with Christian leaders both outside the mainline and outside the traditional ecumenical movement.

To the degree that these denominations are communions (part of the body of Christ) and not merely time- and culture-bound organizational structures, they need to be *resurrected*. Resurrection is not something we can do by ourselves. Resurrection is something that must be accomplished by the Holy Spirit as we open ourselves to being led by the Spirit. Such a resurrection would be for the sake of the core values these bodies represent, not for the sake of us as leaders.

The Way Forward

What might the Holy Spirit be calling us to be and do?

First, whatever else the Spirit may be calling us to be and do, I believe we are being led to rediscover our core values, the ones that remain at our heart as mainline denominations. We just talked about some of those in the last chapter. In the face of our decline since 1968, we have become anxious and, in our anxiety, we have been tempted to sell our birthright for a mess of potage. Let us rediscover who we are and what our gift to the wider Church and world is, bringing our day-to-day life into congruence with these core values, without apology.

Second, whatever else the Spirit may be calling us to do, I believe that God is leading us to move from maintenance to mission. The leap from maintenance to mission is like a trapeze act. We have to let go of the bar we are holding before we are able to grab the new bar. Otherwise, we end up suspended in space, going back and forth in smaller and smaller arcs till we are dead in the air.

What might this moving from maintenance to mission look like?

Establish New Congregations

We need to start new congregations. If we really believe that we have something to offer to the wider church and to the whole world, then we should seek to offer more of it rather than less. We have been offering less and less since 1968, when most of us stopped birthing new congregations or birthed only a handful per year.

It was about that time that we got anxious, started holding on for dear life and, thus, started over-controlling. We developed detailed protocols for how a new congregation might get started to insure that they were started "right" and that each one would succeed. But, lo and behold, such bureaucratic approaches did not guarantee success. They mostly squeezed out the "holy entrepreneurialism" that is necessary to start a church. It is really hard to *administrate* a congregation into being.

Most mainline congregations are now somewhere on the downside of the Congregational Life Cycle (see chapter 4). Some of them are *far* down that side and have become so contextually irrelevant and so low on resources that there is little hope of turning it around. For nearly four decades, we have seen years in which many more congregations have closed or merged away than have been started. "Those who want to save their life will lose it" (Lk. 9:24). We have to *invest* in God's future for these denominations; we can't keep our death grip on everything we are holding onto now and successfully start congregations. We can't insist on starting new congregations only with official approval and bureaucratic oversight by middle judicatories and denominational units. We must push congregation establishment back to where it was when we were all starting so many congregations: to existing congregations themselves. There is no one right way to start new congregations. We must encourage congregations to start them, in some cases middle judicatories will need to start them, in other cases they will be started by entrepreneurial pastors and then we will adopt them into the family. As my friend Rick Morse says, "Start a thousand congregations in a thousand ways!"

Will some of these starts fail? Of course, but the number succeeding will far outstrip the numbers that were started using our old "safer" methods, and the result will be new life for the whole denomination. If you wait to have children until you can afford them, you will never have them. It is a matter of investing in and expanding the mission of each of the mainline denominations.

A disproportionate number of these new congregations (compared with our existing congregations) will need to be racial/ethnic in makeup. Why? Because the population trends tell us that by the year 2030 or so, less than half of Americans will be of Euro-American decent. If the United States is our primary mission field (for doing evangelism, for teaching, and for converting people to the practice of social justice at home and around the globe), then our membership demographics should look very much like the demographics of the United States population itself. Otherwise, something is wrong.

As the proportion of racial/ethnic members increases via new congregation establishment, competing cultural assumptions will cause other kinds of crises. This also happened when the World War II generation came of age and reshaped these churches in the 1950s and 60s. Adaptive change is always provocative, but that's no reason to avoid it.

In order to simply keep even in terms of numbers of congregations, in relation to the ones closing, a denomination must start a number of congregations equal to 3 percent of its current number of congregations each year. But the point here is not, and must not be, saving our institutions. The point must be to expand our mission for the sake of the God who called these churches into being. Yet, it is as the church pours its life out in mission that it finds its life.

Revitalize Existing Congregations

Yes, many of our existing congregations are *far* down the declining side of the Congregational Life Cycle and have become *so* contextually irrelevant that they will turn in on themselves. Without some kind of intervention, they will surely die. But intervention is possible. Intervention may come in the form of a pastor who is mission-motivated and well-trained in organizational dynamics. Intervention may come in the form of consultant-coaches who are asked in. Intervention may come in the form of denominational units and middle judicatories who are prepared to offer assistance. Intervention is likely to come in myriad forms.

Most denominational units and middle judicatories are, frankly, too busy and have too few resources to mount a major intervention effort by themselves. They will serve better and be better served if they network and broker the services of consultant/coaches who are independent contractors or who have been trained by the unit or judicatory for the purpose. This is especially true if they use the services of contractors who are motivated by mission and who are primarily interested in building the capacity of those institutions they serve rather than creating dependence upon themselves as contractors. Whether by a middle judicatory staff person, a coach trained by the middle judicatory, or an independent contractor, congregations need help in regularly revisioning. Congregations need someone to help them keep the three questions before themselves and to hold them accountable to the changes to which they commit themselves.

As has been said, revitalization/transformation is not a destination; it is an ongoing journey. Congregations typically need to refresh their sense of vision about every five to seven years on average. If the denominational units or middle judicatories are going to meet this challenge, then they must offer an approach that engages about one-seventh of their existing congregations every year. (Perhaps one-eighth would be adequate, for some congregations will do it on their own.)

I believe some congregations just need to die, either because they have passed the point of no return or because they have been captured by dynamics that are so negative as to be practically insurmountable. But many congregations can be revitalized or transformed for a productive future. Why simply "write off" existing congregations when some competent intervention could send them toward a new "prime time"?

Confront Racism

As new congregations bring significant numbers of racial-ethnic folks of all kinds into these predominantly Euro-American denominations, our denominations in all expressions must be hospitable and create a safe place for them. This means we must deal with the bigotry (racial prejudice) among our current membership and the very real racism (bigotry expressed systemically) that remains in every mainline denomination's system. This is a matter of integrity as well as mission.

Develop Leaders

In these eight mainline denominations, about two-thirds of those currently serving in ministry will retire within the next fifteen years. My experience is that the Baby Buster generation and the Millennial generations have many people who are bright, idealistic, and willing to explore ministry as a vocation. But we can no longer count on the culture at large to recruit these folks for us. We must take the initiative in identifying the brightest and the best of these young people, meeting them where they are, and challenging them to the possibility of a life of full-time Christian service.

People who feel called to ministry in mid-life often bring extraordinary gifts with them, including practical experience. These folks, too, need encouragement and nurture.

We need to develop more scholarship money for all of these potential candidates for ministry. It is not unusual for students to graduate from seminary with more than $50,000 in debt. We must also take licensed and bivocational ministers more seriously and provide ways for them to consistently upgrade their knowledge and skills.

However, the leadership needs of our churches go beyond effective clergy leaders. We also need to provide Christian education and leadership development for laypeople who have their own ministry and who feel called to lead.

Remember the story of the paralyzed man at the pool of Bethsaida (John 5:2–9)? The tradition was that, when the waters of the pool were stirring, any sick person who was first to reach the water would be healed. The text says this paralytic had been stationed at the pool for thirty-eight years. He had been there all those years and Jesus comes along and asks him what at first blush might seem to be a terribly insensitive question. "Do you want to be healed?" The man must have wanted to say to Jesus: "*Do I want to be healed? Are you crazy?* Why do you think I have been lying around this pool for thirty-eight years waiting for someone to put me in the water at the right moment?"

But instead he explains to Jesus, as he had no doubt explained to so many others who had inquired about his situation, "Sir, I have no one to put me into the pool when the water is stirred up; and while I am making my way, someone steps down ahead of me" (v. 7).

Doesn't this man remind you of so many people, maybe even ourselves? Some of us have been going to church for thirty-eight years, and yet have never changed a bit. Maybe it's because so many of us, when we get the chance, sit at the very back or in the balcony, so that it is harder to really get into the swim of the things of the Spirit. Little danger of transformation exists when you go through all the motions of church yet you are distancing yourself from the stirrings of the Spirit.

Jesus must have wanted to say, "Well, if you can't get to the water while it is stirred up, *maybe you should move from the back of the sanctuary to the edge of the pool!*" But Jesus made his point instead by asking the right question. Even as this man was giving his excuses for why he could not do what the tradition of the pool of Bethsaida said it took to be healed, the saving truth began to dawn on him.

So *now* he could respond with faith and courage when Jesus told him...simply...with authority, "Stand up, take your mat and walk" (v. 8). It was an endorsement of what the man had come to see about himself just a moment before, an endorsement of his sudden recognition that his ability to be healed had nothing to do with that pool of water. "At once the man was made well, and he took up his mat and began to walk" (v. 9).

Jesus asked a powerful question. It was a gentle question, but a question so powerful that it was able to cut through all the man's denial, self-pity, grief, and doubt.

"Do you want to be healed?"

After thirty-eight or so years of anxious hand-wringing, blame-laying, and denial, maybe this is the question Jesus is posing to these eight denominations (and to not a few of the other churches in the body of Christ). Do you want to be healed? Are you ready?

Readiness means becoming aware of how we have been held captive by past circumstances and paradigms, and how these have been driving our churches' life and work. Readiness means opening ourselves to new ways and means and, most of all, taking responsibility for our healing and opening ourselves to the leadership of the Holy Spirit.Dialogue, prayer, Bible study, and learning experiences that focus on inspiration and dreaming can enhance readiness. I am hopeful that this small book will be a contribution to a dialogue that has been intensifying in recent years, and will thus help in creating the readiness we need in the mainline denominations.

This is not the same question as, "Can we be restored to the way we were in 1955?" The answer to this question is no. We can't go back because there is no "there" there.

But can we become *effective* in the world of today? The answer to this question is yes.

Can we be healed? We can be...whenever we are ready, whenever we *want* to be...whenever our "yes" creates an opening for the Spirit to do what only the Spirit can do. Leaning into this "yes" is the only way to live. But expect adaptive change to follow!

We don't have to change everything—just the things that are killing us, just the things that keep us from effectively doing the mission Christ has called us to do.

Questions to Use in Exploring a Context

When I am working with a congregation as a coach/consultant, I ask for the following materials and for answers to the following questions. You may wish to use these as a guide for your own study of the institution you are serving or about to serve.

There is no end to the questions one can ask, but the point is to ask enough questions to help the group get an accurate picture of their institution. If you wish to explore other possible questions to ask, I suggest you secure a copy of Lyle Schaller's book *The Interventionist.*[1] There Dr. Schaller identifies a plethora of possible questions that help to give substance to a conversation about an institution as it presently exists.

Ask to see the following materials. They give clues to how the congregation or other institution operates currently. Terminologies and structures vary from denomination to denomination, so you may need to translate some questions or terms into your tradition's language.

1. Constitution and By-laws
2. Written history of the organization (including a list of the names and tenures of the ministers or executives for the past seventy-five years)
3. Formal policies (personnel, endowment, etc.)
4. Minutes of board meetings for the past three years
5. The annual budgets from five years ago, ten years ago, and fifteen years ago.
6. Annual financial reports for the past ten years (annual summary only)

7. Annual reports to the board or the larger body for each of the past five years (if the organization has annual reports)
8. A street map of the city (in the case of a congregation)
9. The current mission statement (if there is one)
10. The current vision statement (if there is one)
11. The most recent pictorial directory (in the case of a congregation)
12. The most recent nonpictorial directory
13. Copies of the worship bulletins for six representative Sundays of the past year (in the case of a congregation)

Research Questions
(these are for congregations but can be adapted for other church institutions)

1. Approximately how many members were lost during each of the last ten years by death? By transfer due to moving away? By transfer due to dissatisfaction or anger?

2. Secure a flat street map of the metropolitan area to a corkboard and place push pins as follows (different colors may be substituted as available):

   • red push pins wherever there is the residence of a family unit (which includes single-person family units) that participates in the congregation whose head of household is under 30.

   • blue push pins wherever there is the residence of a family unit that participates whose head of household is 30–39.

   • brown push pins wherever there is the residence of a family unit that participates whose head of household is 40–49.

   • green push pins wherever there is the residence of a family unit that participates whose head of household is 50–59.

   • black push pins wherever there is the residence of a family unit that participates whose head of household is 60–69.

   • yellow push pins wherever there is the residence of a family unit that participates whose head of household is 70 or older.

   • white push pins wherever there is the residence of a family unit that belongs but no longer participates.

   Place a key to the meaning of each color on a corner of the map. Also, to denote those participating members who live beyond the boundaries of the map, place an appropriately colored pin at the edge of the map so as to indicate the direction in which they live.

3. Gather age/gender/marital status information for your participating members and sort the data into age categories. Divide children and youth into smaller categories (0–4, 5–9, 10–14, 15–19) and adults into ten-year increments.

4. What percentage of the congregation is (name the predominant racial/ethnic group)? What other groups are present in the congregation and in what percentages?

5. How many participating members have:

   Less than a high school diploma?
   A high school diploma only?
   A college diploma?
   A graduate degree or more?

   (This question, and #6, can be answered through a paper survey conducted at worship over two or three Sundays. Signatures should not be sought, as some may find these questions embarrassing. Though you will not get information for every single member, you will get information for the great majority, and percentages can be applied to the total membership for a reasonably accurate picture.)

6. How many participating members who work outside the home have employment in each of the following categories (choose only one per person):

   farmer _____   teacher _____
   laborer_____   school administrator _____
   clerical _____   health care professional _____
   middle management _____ upper management _____
   service provider _____ other _____

   (In your particular community, there may be other categories that need to be added. If your congregation has a significant number of retired persons, indicate how many are retired from each category above.)

7. Over the past fifteen years, what has been the length of tenure of individual church secretaries, custodians, associate ministers, staff musicians, senior ministers, other staff (by name).

8. Please name those small groups in the life of the church in which membership is emotionally significant and how many participants are in each. For example, participation in the adult choir, children's choir, bell choir, a Sunday school class, women's circles, etc. is emotionally significant. Participation in groups that do not meet or in which members do not communicate with each other, such as a "shepherding group" that does not meet together is not emotionally significant.

9. How many members are on the general board (or other governing body)? If there is a cabinet or similar executive committee type of group, how many are on it? How many departments and/or committees are there (please name) and how many members serve on each? How often does each of these groups meet?

Questions to Be Answered by a Visioning Committee Together
(or by another group of members brought together for the purpose)

1. What do you call the laypeople who provide primary spiritual leadership for your congregation and what do they do?
2. When it comes to evangelism, what do you consider the geographical target area of the congregation to be?
3. When you think of local outreach, what do you consider the geographical target area of the congregation to be?
4. What outreach projects/programs has the congregation undertaken within the past ten years and how many of these projects/programs are currently active?
5. In order of importance, list the reasons why you as individual committee members think participating members attend your congregation? (Do not seek to come to a consensus on this list, but brainstorm the possible reasons and then ask the individual members of the committee to indicate what they think are the five most important reasons. After each category, please place the number of committee members who voted for each—with a maximum of five votes for each member of the committee.)
6. Brainstorm a list of all the things your congregation does as a church. By consensus, what are the six things the committee believes your congregation does best? What are the six things the committee believes your congregation does least well?
7. Describe the women's group or groups:
8. Describe the men's group or groups:
9. Describe the youth group or groups currently and over the past five-to-ten years:
10. Are there signs of renewal in the congregation that you wish to name?
11. Are there signs of decline you wish to name?
12. How would you describe the self-image of the congregation?
13. Have there been serious conflicts in the life of the congregation during the past twenty-five years? If so, please describe.
14. Has a committee identified a list of capital needs, improvements, or repairs that need to be addressed? If so, please identify these items and the committee(s) that have identified them.
15. What percentage of governing board members attend board meetings typically? What percentage of committee members attend committee meetings typically?
16. Which committees/departments would you describe as functioning and healthy? Which would you describe as nonfunctioning and not healthy?
17. Please describe your city economically, politically, socially, religiously, attitudinally, etc.
18. Is there anything else you think the congregation should know about itself or the community?

Notes

Preface

[1]My advice to them is to make their words soft and palatable, for they never know when they may find themselves called to ministry in one of the other expressions.

[2]For example, George W. Bullard's book *Pursuing the Full Kingdom Potential of Your Congregation* (St. Louis: Lake Hickory Resources, 2005) is a marvelous resource for those who are seeking to effectively lead churches into the postmodern era.

[3]Dorothy C. Bass, "Reflections on the Reports of Decline in Mainstream Protestantism," *Chicago Theological Register* 80, no. 3 (summer 1989): 5–15 (see note 1, p. 14).

Chapter 1: Why Is Leadership in the Mainline Church So Difficult?

[1]"If any want to become my followers, let them deny themselves and take up their cross daily and follow me" (Lk. 9:23).

[2]Ephesians 3:10 and Colossians 3:15 (RSV).

[3]"And after six days Jesus took with him Peter and James and John his brother, and led them up a high mountain apart. And he was transfigured before them, and his face shone like the sun, and his garments became white as light. And behold, there appeared to them Moses and Elijah, talking with him. And Peter said to Jesus, 'Lord, it is well that we are here; if you wish, I will make three booths here, one for you and one for Moses and one for Elijah.' He was still speaking, when lo, a bright cloud overshadowed them, and a voice from the cloud said, 'This is my beloved Son with whom I am well pleased; listen to him.' When the disciples heard this, they fell on their faces, and were filled with awe" (RSV).

Chapter 2: Technical and Adaptive Change

[1]Ron Heiftez, *Leadership Without Easy Answers* (Cambridge, Mass.: Belknap Press of Harvard Univ. Press, 1994).

[2]For an accounting of the value of these mainline traditions, see chapter 11: "Why Bother?"

[3]Heifetz, *Leadership Without Easy Answers*, 66f.

Part I: How Did It Come to This?

[1]George Santayana, *Reason in Common Sense*, 1905 (available free online from "Project Gutenberg").

Chapter 4: The Second Element of the Perfect Storm

[1]For example, the United Methodist Church rode a powerful wave of expressed spirituality; the Christian Church (Disciples of Christ) rode a wave of individual freedom on the American frontier.

[2]George Bullard is a church consultant, a coach, and a partner with me in The Columbia Partnership. I recommend his excellent book, *Pursuing the Full Kingdom Potential of Your Congregation* (St. Louis: Lake Hickory Resources, 2005).

[3]Arlin J. Rothauge, "Sizing Up a Congregation for New Member Ministry" (New York: Episcopal Church Center, 1983).

Chapter 5: The Third Element of the Perfect Storm

[1]I commend the writings of Thomas Friedman, editorial writer for *The New York Times*. See, e.g., his books: *The Lexus and the Olive Tree* (New York: First Anchor Books, 2000) and *The World Is Flat* (New York: Farrar, Straus and Giroux, 2005).

127

[2]Systems do not actually have a "center of will," as an individual does, of course. Paul Tillich wrote *Love, Power, and Justice* (Oxford: Oxford University Press, 1960) to address this very matter. "Systems" cannot feel or decide. However, it often *seems* as if systems can feel and decide. Although I have studied systems for years, there is yet an element of mystery about them for me. It is akin to the "principalities and powers" of which Paul speaks (RSV). While much popular religion focuses on good and evil as it is expressed in the lives of individuals, I believe any mature understanding of the world must take seriously the way good and evil are expressed through *systems*. As individuals, systems, for good or ill, use us in ways we seldom fully understand or appreciate. We Americans tend to be particularly naïve about these matters as our culture is so deeply immersed in radical individualism. In a system, 2 + 2 equals much *more* than four.

[3]G. Lloyd Rediger, *Clergy Killers: Guidance for Pastors and Congregations Under Attack* (Louisville: Westminster John Knox Press, 1997).

[4]Edwin H. Friedman, *Generation to Generation: Family Process in Church and Synagogue* (New York: The Guildford Press, 1985), 39.

[5]Ron Heifetz, *Leadership Without Easy Answers* (Cambridge: Belknap Press of Harvard University Press, 1994), 103f.

Chapter 6: Generational Differences

[1]One of the examples of sacrifices made by others, which often surprises Americans who learn of it, involves the celebrated "Doolittle Raid." Early in the war (April 1942), in order to boost American morale back home in the wake of Pearl Harbor, to bring the war "home" to the Japanese, and to force the Japanese to use soldiers to defend the homeland, Colonel Jimmy Doolittle led an attack force of B-25s from an aircraft carrier to bomb Tokyo. It was a daring undertaking, and in the process, nine of the American airmen were killed or captured. However, most Americans are unaware that some 250,000 Chinese were killed because they harbored (or were suspected of harboring) American airmen whose B-25s went down in Japanese-controlled China.

[2]Robert S. McNamara with Brian VanDeMark, *In Retrospect: The Tragedy and Lessons of Vietnam* (New York: Random House, 1995).

Chapter 7: The Crisis in Governance of Mainline Churches

[1]These participatory structures were put in place in reaction to more autocratic forms of government that characterized many institutions before WWII.

Chapter 8: Seeing the Challenges through Polarities

[1]William McKinney, ed., *The Responsibility People* (Grand Rapids: Eerdmans, 1994).

[2]We do well to remember and review Richard Niebuhr's categories: Christ *against* culture, Christ *of* culture, Christ *above* culture, Christ and culture in *paradox*, and Christ the *transformer* of culture. See H. Richard Niebuhr, *Christ and Culture* (New York: Harper and Row, 1951). Niebuhr (1894–1962) was a twentieth-century American Protestant theologian and churchman known especially for his writings on Christian ethics and his social analysis of American denominationalism.

Chapter 9: Personal Aspects of Leading Adaptive Change

[1]Stephen Hill included "The Tables Turned," a poem written in 1798, in his collection of works by William Wordsworth, titled *The Major Works: Including The Prelude* (Oxford: The Oxford University Press, 2000), 130.

[2]The notable exception to this was Coach Dan Thomas, who I believe was more interested in character development than in the score at the end of our junior high basketball games. I owe this educator much for helping me through a very difficult passage in my life.

[3]Addressed by Loren Mead in his book *Financial Meltdown in the Mainline?* (Washington, D.C.: Alban Institute, 1998).

[4]Robert Fulghum, *It Was on Fire When I Lay Down on It* (New York: Ivy Books of Ballantine Books, Random House, 1988).

Chapter 10: Systemic Aspects of Leading Adaptive Change

[1]Jim Collins, *Good To Great* (New York: HarperCollins, 2001).

[2]Elton Trueblood, *The Predicament of Modern Man* (Burlingame, Calif.: Yokefellow Press, 1984), 59.

[3]Ezekiel 37.

[4]Albert C. Outler, *John Wesley* (New York: Oxford University Press, 1964).

[5]While the vast majority of both middle judicatory and national leaders of denominations are people of integrity and skill, it must be admitted that, given the typical denominational structures in mainline churches, any judicatory or national executive who isn't smart enough to keep meaningful criticism at bay isn't smart enough to be a head of such a structure to start with. Unfortunately, this means that most of those who are unwittingly being used by the system to evade effective adaptive change are very effective dupes for homeostasis.

Chapter 11: Why Bother?

[1]While it may be argued that mainline denominational schools were originally established for the purpose of indoctrination, it is a reflection of the maturation of mainline Christian educators that they responded to the challenges of modernism in the early twentieth century with a commitment to seek truth rather than remaining doctrinaire. See Dorothy C. Bass's article "Teaching with Authority?: The Changing Place of Mainstream Protestantism in American Culture," *Religious Education* 85, no. 2 (Spring 1990): 295–310, for a helpful discussion of the change in our educational institutions and their context.

[2]Although a smaller proportion of denominational offerings are going to support these liberal arts institutions, most of the individual donors upon which these schools are so dependent are willing to contribute primarily because their mainline denomination/congregation has taught them to do so.

Appendix: Questions to Use in Exploring a Context

[1]Lyle Schaller, *The Interventionist* (Nashville: Abingdon Press, 1997).

Bibliography

Bullard, George W., Jr. *Pursuing the Full Kingdom Potential of Your Congregation*. St. Louis: Lake Hickory Resources, 2005.

Collins, Jim. *Good To Great*. New York: HarperCollins, 2001.

Friedman, Edwin. *A Failure of Nerve*. Bethesda, Md.: The Edwin Friedman Estate/Trust, 1999.

———. *Generation to Generation: Family Process in Church and Synagogue*. New York: The Guilford Press, 1985.

Friedman, Thomas L. *The Lexus and the Olive Tree*. New York: First Anchor Book Edition, Random House, 2000.

———. *The World Is Flat*. New York: Farrar, Straus and Giroux, 2005.

Fulghum, Robert. *It Was on Fire When I Lay Down on It*. New York: Ivy Books of Ballantine Books, Random House, 1988.

Goleman, Daniel, Richard Boyatzis, Annie McKee. *Primal Leadership*. Boston: Harvard Business School Press, 2002.

Heifetz, Ronald. *Leadership Without Easy Answers*. Cambridge: Belknap Press of Harvard University Press, 1994.

Junger, Sebastian. *The Perfect Storm*. New York: W.W. Norton & Co, 1997.

McKinney, William, ed. *The Responsibility People*. Grand Rapids: Eerdmans, 1994.

McNamara, Robert S., with Brian VanDeMark. *In Retrospect: The Tragedy and Lessons of Vietnam*. New York: Random House, 1995.

Mead, Loren. *Financial Meltdown in the Mainline?* Washington, D.C.: Alban Institute, 1998.

Morris, Danny, and Charles Olsen. *Discerning God's Will Together: A Spiritual Practice for the Church*. Nashville: Upper Room Books, 1997.

Niebuhr, H. Richard. *Christ and Culture*. New York: Harper and Row, 1951.

Rediger, G. Lloyd. *Clergy Killers: Guidance for Pastors and Congregations under Attack*. Louisville: Westminster John Knox Press, 1997.

Rendle, Gilbert R., and Alice Mann. *Holy Conversations: Strategic Planning as a Spiritual Practice for Congregations*. Bethesda, Md.: Alban Institute, 2003.

Schaller, Lyle. *The Interventionist*. Nashville: Abingdon Press, 1997.

Tillich, Paul. *Love, Power and Justice*. London: Oxford University Press, 1954.

Trueblood, Elton. *The Predicament of Modern Man*. Burlingame, Calif.: Yokefellow Press, 1984.